Monetary and Financial Integration in East Asia

Monetary and Financial Integration in East Asia

The Way Ahead: Volume 1

Edited by

Asian Development Bank

palgrave
macmillan

First published 2004 by
PALGRAVE MACMILLAN
Houndmills, Basingstoke, Hampshire RG21 6XS and
175 Fifth Avenue, New York, N. Y. 10010
Companies and representatives throughout the world

PALGRAVE MACMILLAN is the global academic imprint of the Palgrave Macmillan division of St. Martin's Press, LLC and of Palgrave Macmillan Ltd. Macmillan® is a registered trademark in the United States, United Kingdom and other countries. Palgrave is a registered trademark in the European Union and other countries.

ISBN 1–4039–1882–1

This book is printed on paper suitable for recycling and made from fully managed and sustained forest sources.

A catalogue record for this book is available from the British Library.

Library of Congress Cataloging-in-Publication Data

Monetary and financial integration in East Asia : the way ahead / edited by Asian Development Bank.
p. cm.
Includes bibliographical references and index.
ISBN 1–4039–1882–1 (v. 1) -- ISBN 1–4039–2086–9 (v. 2)
1. Monetary unions--East Asia. 2. Monetary policy--East Asia. 3. Foreign exchange rates--East Asia. 4. East Asia--Economic integration. I. Asian Development Bank.

HG1270.5.M66 2004
332'.042'095--dc22

2003060959

10 9 8 7 6 5 4 3 2 1
13 12 11 10 09 08 07 06 05 04

Printed and bound in Great Britain by
Antony Rowe Ltd, Chippenham and Eastbourne

Contents

Tables and Figures

Tables

Figure

Foreword

Since the 1997 Asian financial crisis, there have been several important initiatives for regional monetary and financial cooperation in East Asia. In October 1998, the ASEAN finance ministers established the ASEAN Surveillance Process. Under this Process, the ministers and their deputies meet semiannually to exchange information, undertake peer review of economic policies, and consider individual and collective responses to events that could impact adversely on the region. In November 1999, the ASEAN+3 Finance Ministers Process was formalized. Under this Process, the ministers and their deputies meet semiannually to review the emerging global and regional economic situation and discuss policy challenges. In May 2000, the ASEAN+3 finance ministers announced the Chiang Mai Initiative. The proponents agreed to extend financial assistance to member countries through a network of bilateral currency swap agreements. In their January 2001 meeting in Kobe, Japan, the Asia-Europe finance ministers decided to encourage cooperative activities in the economic and financial fields among Asian and European countries. As a first step, the ministers launched the Kobe Research Project (KRP) that was intended to facilitate cooperative research by Asian and European institutions and experts, and to cover broad thematic areas including regional cooperation. Under the KRP, several studies were undertaken to explore ways of improving regional monetary and financial cooperation.

These initiatives at the regional level have complemented policies and actions at the national and global levels in improving not only the resilience of the region to economic shocks but also its ability to manage shocks that may occur. Going forward, the key issue is how these initiatives for regional monetary and financial cooperation should be sequenced and at what speed they should proceed. This two-volume book addresses this issue.

The book comprises core reports and background papers by eminent economists and policymakers around the world commissioned under the Asian Development Bank (ADB) Study on Monetary and Financial Cooperation in East Asia. The preliminary findings of the Study, which was ADB's major contribution to the KRP, were presented to the Asia-Europe finance ministers in their July 2002 meeting.

The book explores what is feasible and desirable in regional monetary and financial cooperation, and lays out a road map of policy options for putting the concept into action over the next several years. In particular, it addresses the following questions: Is there merit in formalizing and intensifying the process of regional information exchange and surveillance? Should the bilateral currency swap arrangements of the Chiang Mai Initiative be expanded and multilateralized? Should a centralized reserve pooling arrangement at the regional level be established? If so, what should be the approximate size of such a centralized reserve pool, and who should have responsibility for managing the reserve pool? Should countries in the region aim at exchange rate policy coordination; if so, what form should such coordination take? How can it be ensured that all these regional initiatives—be they in the area of economic surveillance, reserve pooling, or exchange rate coordination—complement initiatives at the global level? How best can countries in the region cooperate in the area of financial sector reforms and restructuring—an area that has become critical in the postcrisis years?

After extensive analysis of these issues, the book lays out recommendations for feasible and desirable forms of enhanced cooperation and actions for the short (within the next 2 years), medium (3–5 years), and longer term (over 5 years). In coming up with the recommendations, the overarching concern has been to ensure that attempts to build a new regional financial architecture in Asia do not run counter to the international financial architecture that is being nurtured globally by various institutions. The objective is to complement global activities with regional initiatives. This perspective is crucial because regional efforts should form the building blocks for global initiatives. Carefully designed regional initiatives and their appropriate sequencing are needed to ensure the complementarity of global and regional efforts. The book will be of value to a wide spectrum of users—academics, policymakers, governments, development institutions, students of economics, and the general public—who are interested in regional monetary and financial cooperation initiatives and policy options for East Asia.

Tadao Chino
President
Asian Development Bank

Acknowledgments

The collection of core studies and background papers in this two-volume book was prepared as part of the Asian Development Bank's technical assistance project, A Study on Monetary and Financial Cooperation in East Asia. Under the overall guidance of Yoshihiro Iwasaki, Head of the Regional Economic Monitoring Unit (REMU), the project was conceptualized, supervised, and coordinated by Pradumna B. Rana and Srinivasa Madhur. Adrian Panggabean assisted in the administration of the project. Peter J. Montiel was economics editor of the core studies in Volume 1; Graham James Dwyer and Gloria Argosino were the copy editors. Wilhelmina Paz provided technical and research support, Elizabeth Leuterio Aspin provided manuscript reading services, and Segundo dela Cruz, Jr. typeset the papers and conceptualized the book and cover design. Lilibeth Perez and Rosario Razon provided secretarial support.

Contributors

Volume 1

Olarn Chaipravat
Fiscal Policy Research Institute
Thailand

Eric Girardin
Centre de Recherches sur les Dynamiques, les Politiques Economiques et l'Economie des Ressources (CEDERS)
Université de la Mediterranée, Aix-Marseille II
France

Takatoshi Ito
Research Center for Advanced Science and Technology
University of Tokyo
Japan

Peter J. Montiel
Department of Economics
Williams College
The United States

Yung Chul Park
Department of Economics
Korea University
The Republic of Korea

Volume 2

Robert J. Barro
Department of Economics
Harvard University
The United States

Eléonore Boiscuvier
Institut Univérsitaire de Luxembourg

Barry Eichengreen
Department of Economics
University of California, Berkeley
The United States

Jeffrey A. Frankel
Kennedy School of Government
Harvard University
The United States

Eric Girardin
CEDERS
Université de la Mediterranée, Aix-Marseille II
France

Takatoshi Ito
Research Center for Advanced Science and Technology
University of Tokyo
Japan

Jong-Wha Lee
Department of Economics
Korea University
The Republic of Korea

Ronald I. McKinnon
Department of Economics
Stanford University, California
The United States

Eiji Ogawa
Graduate School of Commerce and Management
Hitotsubashi University
Japan

Yung Chul Park
Department of Economics
Korea University
The Republic of Korea

Ramkishen Rajan
Centre for International Economic Studies
University of Adelaide
Australia

Yuri Nagataki Sasaki
Department of Economics
Meiji Gakuin University
Japan

Kwanho Shin
Department of Economics
Korea University
The Republic of Korea

Reza Siregar
School of Economics
University of Adelaide
Australia

Alfred Steinherr
European Investment Bank
Luxembourg

Yunjong Wang
Korea Institute for International Policy
The Republic of Korea

Wing Thye Woo
Department of Economics
University of California, Davis
The United States

Charles Wyplosz
Graduate Institute of International Studies and International Center for Monetary and Banking Studies (ICMB)
Switzerland

Abbreviations

AAB	ASEAN arrangement to borrow
ACB	Asian Central Bank
ACBF	ASEAN Central Banks Forum
ACCA	Asian common currency area
ACF	Asian Currency Fund
ACU	Asian currency unit
ADB	Asian Development Bank
AEM	ASEAN Economic Ministers
AFDM	ASEAN Finance and Central Bank Deputies Meeting
AFI	Asian Financial Institute
AFMM	ASEAN Finance Ministers' Meeting
AFTA	ASEAN Free Trade Area
AMCF	ASEAN Monetary Cooperation Fund
AMF	Asian Monetary Fund
AMS	Asian monetary system
AMU	Asian monetary unit
APEC	Asia-Pacific Economic Cooperation
ARIC	Asia Recovery Information Center
ASA	ASEAN swap arrangement (agreement)
ASCU	ASEAN Surveillance Coordination Unit
ASEAN	Association of Southeast Asian Nations comprising Brunei Darussalam, Cambodia, Indonesia, Lao People's Democratic Republic, Malaysia, Myanmar, Philippines, Singapore, Thailand, and Viet Nam
ASP	ASEAN Surveillance Process
BAC	Banking Advisory Committee
BBC	basket, band and crawl
BCBS	Basel Committee on Banking Supervision
BCEAO	Banque Centrale des Etats de l'Afrique de l'Ouest
BEAC	Banque Centrale des Etats de l'Afrique Centrale
BEPG	Broad Economic Policy Guidelines

BIS	Bank for International Settlements
BNM	Bank Negara Malaysia
BOT	Bank of Thailand
BSA	bilateral swap agreement (arrangement)
BSC	Banking Supervision Committee
CAEMC	Central African Economic and Monetary Community
CAMEL	capital, asset quality, management, earnings, and liquidity
CAR	capital asset ratio
CCA	common currency area
CCL	contingent credit line
CEPR	Centre for Economic Policy Research
CFA	Communauté Financière Africaine; Communauté Financière de l'Afrique; Cooperation Financière Africaine
CMI	Chiang Mai Initiative
CPI	consumer price index
CVML	Cambodia, Viet Nam, Myanmar, and Lao People's Democratic Republic
DM	deutsche mark
EA-7	People's Republic of China, Indonesia, Japan, Republic of Korea, Malaysia, Singapore, Thailand
EABAC	East Asian Banking Advisory Committee
EARFA	East Asian Regional Financial Arrangement
East Asia	ASEAN plus People's Republic of China, Japan, and Republic of Korea
EAVG	East Asian Vision Group
EC-12	Belgium, Denmark, France, Germany, Greece, Ireland, Italy, Luxembourg, Netherlands, Portugal, Spain, and United Kingdom
ECB	European Central Bank
ECCA	Eastern Caribbean Currency Area
ECOFIN	Council of Ministers of Economics and Finance
ECU	European currency unit
EEC	European Economic Community

EMCF	European Monetary Cooperation Fund
EMEAP	Executive Meeting of East Asian and Pacific Central Banks
EMI	European Monetary Institute
EMS	European Monetary System
EMU	European Monetary Union
EPG	Eminent Persons' Group
EPU	European Payments Union
ERM	exchange rate mechanism
ESCB	European System of Central Banks
EU	European Union
euro-11	The 11 European countries that replaced their national currencies with the euro
FDI	foreign direct investment
FECOM	European Monetary Cooperation Fund
FIDF	Financial Institutions Development Fund
FLAR	Latin American Reserve Fund
FRC	Financial Reconstruction Commission
FSA	financial supervisory authority
FSAP	financial sector assessment program
FSF	Financial Stability Forum
FSM	financial support mechanism
FTA	free trade area
G-3	Europe, Japan, United States
G-8	Canada, France, Germany, Italy, Japan, Russia, United Kingdom, United States
GAB	general agreement to borrow
GATT	General Agreement on Tariffs and Trade
GdeC	Groupe de Contact
GDP	gross domestic product
G-PPP	Generalized Purchasing Power Parity Model
HICP	harmonized index of consumer prices
Hong Kong SAR	Hong Kong Special Administrative Region
IAIS	International Association of Insurance Supervisors
IMF	International Monetary Fund
IOSCO	International Organization of Securities Commissions

ITO	International Trade Organization
Korea	Republic of Korea
KRP	Kobe Research Project
Lao PDR	Lao People's Democratic Republic
LIBOR	London interbank offered rate
LYS	Levy-Yeyati and Sturzenegger
M&A	mergers and acquisitions
MAS	Monetary Authority of Singapore
MBSEA	meetings of banking supervisors of East Asian countries
MCI	monetary conditions index
MFG	Manila Framework Group
MOF	Ministry of Finance
MOU	memorandum of understanding
MTFA	medium-term financial assistance
NAB	new arrangement to borrow
NAFTA	North American Free Trade Agreement
NBER	National Bureau of Economic Research
NCB	national central bank
NEA	North East Asia
NIE	newly industrialized economy
OCA	optimal currency area
OCZ	optimal currency zone
OECD	Organisation for Economic Co-operation and Development
OEEC	Organization for European Economic Cooperation
OLS	ordinary least squares
PPP	purchasing power parity
PRC	People's Republic of China
PTT	Petroleum Authority of Thailand
REMU	Regional Economic Monitoring Unit, ADB
repo	bilateral repurchase agreement
RFA	regional financial arrangement
R/M	reserves-imports ratio
R/STED	ratio of reserves to short-term external debt
RTGS	real-time gross settlement
SEACEN	Southeast Asian Central Banks

SEANZA	Southeast Asia, New Zealand, Australia
SER	stable exchange rate
SGP	Stability and Growth Pact
SOM	senior officials' meeting
STED	short-term external debt
STMS	short-term monetary support
TARGET	Trans-European Automated Real-Time Gross Settlement Express Transfer
UK	The United Kingdom
US	The United States
VSTFF	very short-term financing facility
WAEMU	West African Economic and Monetary Union
WB	World Bank
WDI	World Development Indicators
WG	working group
WPI	wholesale price index
WTO	World Trade Organization

Note: In this volume, "$" refers to US dollars.

1 An overview of monetary and financial integration in East Asia

PETER J. MONTIEL

In the wake of the 1997 Asian financial crisis, interest within the region in enhanced economic cooperation has reached a new peak. The Association of Southeast Asian Nations (ASEAN)+3 summit in Manila in November 1999 gave official support to efforts to develop new forms of cooperation among the 13 countries that attended.[1] The scope of possible areas of cooperation is quite broad and its potential intensity is surprisingly deep, encompassing, among other aspects, the possibility of an eventual Asian monetary union. The reasons for this newly intensified interest in economic cooperation are various, but their root is in the traumatic experience that the Asian crisis represented for the former "miracle" economies of the region.

While the Asian economic miracle was based on a strong outward orientation in economic affairs, it tended to be directed toward the large markets in the industrial countries, rather than within the region itself. Thus, this emerging interest in regional cooperation in Asia in some ways represents a significant break from the recent past. Because of its novelty, the key challenge is how to find a way forward—i.e., how to set priorities and

[1] The group consisted of the 10 members of ASEAN (Brunei Darussalam, Cambodia, Indonesia, Lao People's Democratic Republic, Malaysia, Myanmar, Philippines, Singapore, Thailand, and Viet Nam) plus the People's Republic of China, Japan, and Republic of Korea.

sequence developments to smoothen the path toward a new regional economic framework. This overview study takes up this issue within the context of cooperation on monetary and financial affairs. Building on a series of background papers and core studies prepared for the Asian Development Bank (ADB) Study on Monetary and Financial Cooperation in East Asia, it considers the case for expanding monetary and financial cooperation in the region. It also explores what may be feasible and desirable in economic cooperation, laying out a road map for putting the concept into action over the next several years.

The structure of the report is as follows: the next section examines the reasons for the intensified interest in economic cooperation within Asia. The section that follows then considers the forms that cooperation could take. A distinction is drawn between cooperation on macroeconomic policies and that on financial sector reform and development. In macroeconomics, at the most general level, cooperation could involve sharing information and mutual surveillance over policies; pooling and sharing foreign exchange reserves; and coordinating economic policies around a common regional exchange rate arrangement including, at the extreme, regional monetary unification. The next three sections take up each of these themes in turn. The case for cooperation in financial sector reform and development is then considered. The final section lays out recommendations for feasible and desirable forms of enhanced economic cooperation in Asia and actions that could be undertaken in the short, medium, and long term.

Why cooperate?

To evaluate the potential for and desirability of enhanced economic cooperation in Asia, it is important to understand the factors that are driving the increased interest in this topic among policymakers in the region. The main impetus stems from the Asian financial crisis.

At the most fundamental level, the cross-country contagion that accompanied the crisis suggested that financial crises in one country should not be matters of indifference to the rest. These perceived macroeconomic externalities provide obvious grounds for taking an interest in the macroeconomic policies employed by other Asian countries. Regional cooperation in the monetary and financial spheres represents an obvious way of providing a mechanism for internalizing such macroeconomic externalities.

Aside from regional contagion, specific aspects of the crisis have motivated the desire to explore cooperation in economic policy formulation, as detailed below.

Spillovers from exchange rate policies

One view on the emergence and spread of the crisis in Asia is that exchange rate policies in one country can have significant effects on the economic prospects of others in the region. It holds that Asian countries have been trading increasingly with each other in recent years, while their export products often compete in third markets. Therefore, this perspective places a strong emphasis on the beneficial effects of exchange rate coordination.

The argument is that vulnerability arose because, prior to the crisis, many Asian countries operated de facto dollar pegs, although their trade was relatively diversified geographically. This made them vulnerable to fluctuations in the relative values of G-3 (Europe, Japan, and United States [US]) currencies. This situation is perceived as the outcome of a Nash noncooperative equilibrium, in the sense that, while a basket peg would have been superior for all countries (i.e., it would have provided them with better insulation from G-3 currency fluctuations), trade interdependencies caused dollar pegs to be perceived by each country as individually optimal as long as other countries were doing the same. Thus, the de facto precrisis pegs represented an inferior noncooperative equilibrium. This perspective also concerns the mechanisms that account for the spread of the crisis. Specifically, contagion was also the result of uncoordinated exchange rate policies and occurred through trade channels, at least in part as the result of competitive devaluations.

This interpretation of the emergence and spread of the Asian crisis suggests that mechanisms for coordinating exchange rate policy within the region may have the potential to deliver superior cooperative equilibria in the future. Coordination, in turn, would motivate harmonization of other areas of macroeconomic policy—specifically, in monetary policy formulation.

Inadequate supplies of international liquidity

A second motivation has been provided by the crisis-borne perception that access to large stocks of liquid resources can help protect individual countries from disruptive capital outflows that culminate in currency crises. This has been coupled with the simultaneous perception that existing international mechanisms for liquidity support (led by the International Monetary Fund [IMF]) may have been inadequate for Asian countries. They were accompanied by macroeconomic conditionality that some observers both within the region and outside considered to be inappropriate.

Since the crisis, several Asian countries have accumulated large stocks of liquid foreign exchange reserves. Since reserve accumulation is expensive, the desire to economize on such reserves by pooling them among like-minded countries has provided a separate justification for macroeconomic coordination.[2] Designing mechanisms for reserve pooling, as well as criteria for making pooled reserves available to participating countries, involves macroeconomic coordination.

Common financial sector vulnerabilities

The conventional diagnosis for the structural roots of the crisis, which gave birth to the international community's postcrisis policy agenda for the region, has provided yet a third motive for enhanced cooperation within Asia, in this case in the financial arena. Specifically, the crisis was perceived as having its origins in

---

[2] While the importance attached to reserve adequacy is consistent with a "panic" interpretation of the crisis, it does not necessarily presuppose such an interpretation, since the role of reserves is also important in multiple-equilibrium interpretations. Under the latter type of interpretation, a large reserve stock can shrink the zone of vulnerability within which a country is susceptible to a speculative attack.

weaknesses in the financial sector and corporate governance. Most of the postcrisis reform agenda has focused on structural reforms. Since the diagnosis of the problem has many common elements across countries, and since the postcrisis policies that have been advocated therefore also have much in common, some observers have concluded that cross-country cooperation on reform may be beneficial.

Regional contagion may have provided the general motivation for a new and intense interest in coordination within Asia, while each of the three factors listed above sparked interest in coordination along specific dimensions. But interest has also been fanned by one additional factor: the successful example of western Europe, culminating in the introduction of the euro in January 2001. The European experience not only may have demonstrated that disparate countries can achieve a high degree of cooperation, but also potentially offers a road map for Asian countries to follow.

Varieties of economic coordination

All of these motives suggest that monetary and financial cooperation may be both feasible and beneficial for Asian countries. But such cooperation can take many forms, and the various motives just outlined actually imply very different types of cooperation. As a first step, it is useful to consider how these various motives map into the different forms that enhanced cooperation could take.

Cooperation in the monetary (macroeconomic) and financial (structural) areas can be considered separately. This is not to imply that they are independent. Increased cooperation in one of these areas is likely to promote cooperation in the other.[3] But it is certainly *possible* to cooperate more intensively on macroeconomic matters while pursuing the financial sector reform agenda on a country-by-country basis, or to consult and pool resources on the

[3] The core study by Ito and Park (this volume), for example, makes the point that enhanced cooperation in financial sector reform may promote exchange rate coordination.

financial sector reform process without coordinating macroeconomic policies.

Accordingly, cooperation and coordination in these two areas will be treated separately in the sections that follow. The remainder of this section will consider the various forms that macroeconomic coordination can take and how these relate to the motives for coordination outlined above. The discussion of coordination in financial reform and development is reserved for separate treatment in a later section.

The various forms of macroeconomic coordination that could be contemplated within Asia can be related to each other in a systematic way. Specifically, one can imagine a range of different types of coordination that vary in intensity, in the sense that they involve progressively increasing constraints on the amount of discretion that each country can exercise in designing its own macroeconomic policies. The types of coordination are given below in order of intensity.

Information coordination and surveillance

The weakest form of macroeconomic cooperation involves simply sharing information. Improved flows of economic information among interdependent countries can be welfare-enhancing, because they allow individual countries to make (unconstrained) policy choices in a more informed environment. This form can be carried out in various ways that involve the development of progressively increasing regional expertise in processing macroeconomic information. It can involve the sharing of information already provided to international institutions on a confidential basis, the preparation by national authorities of new reports on country circumstances to be shared with other countries, or filtering the information through a new regional monitoring agency. But this form of information sharing does not involve any attempt by countries to influence the macroeconomic policies of others. We can refer to this weakest form of information sharing simply as "information coordination."

A stronger form of coordination focusing on sharing information would involve discussing such reports in a joint forum, providing an opportunity for exerting "peer pressure" to dissuade individual countries from a course of policy action that may be perceived as harmful to others. Since this form would involve creating an explicit mechanism for individual countries to exert pressure on others, to distinguish it from the pure sharing of information we can refer to it as "surveillance." This remains a form of information coordination, however, in the sense that it simply makes the information flow bidirectional—i.e., countries share information on their circumstances and policy intentions and receive feedback from other countries. Under an arrangement of this type, there are neither economic "carrots" nor "sticks" deployed by the participating countries to influence the behavior of any particular country. The model for this type of forum may resemble the biannual G-8 (Canada, France, Germany, Italy, Japan, Russia, United Kingdom, and US) policy discussions.

This type of coordination most directly responds to the concern with regional contagion as a driving force for economic coordination within Asia. Frequent consultation and information sharing among policymakers will, at least potentially, allow countries to adopt protective measures in anticipation of potential crises elsewhere. It also provides technical assistance and exerts influence designed to induce a potential crisis-prone country to moderate its policies to avoid any crisis.

Resource coordination (reserve pooling)

A stronger form of coordination consists of sharing foreign exchange reserves to take advantage of the benefits of resource pooling (this can be referred to as "resource coordination"). This can take a variety of forms. There is the negotiation of temporary ad hoc bilateral swap arrangements between countries in limited amounts, with short maturities; restricted options for renewal; and conditionality determined by an external agency and available only at the discretion of the country that provides the "hard" currency in the transaction. It can also embrace the creation of a permanent common reserve pool containing large amounts of resources administered by a permanent regional secretariat that determines the conditions for drawing on the pool and with ultimate decisions on disbursing funds made multilaterally. The model for the weaker form of resource pooling is the ASEAN Swap Arrangement (ASA), while the stronger form is represented by IMF as currently constituted (i.e., under the post-Jamaica Agreement).

Resource coordination is predicated on bilateral information flows. Such flows are required both to allow decisions on the disbursement of funds to be made and to design appropriate conditionality for their use—i.e., to cope with the adverse selection and moral hazard problems associated with any kind of lending. But the ability to extend or withhold liquidity assistance appends to information flows a "carrot and stick" aspect that allows participating countries collectively to influence the behavior of individual countries in the group. This property, together with the more extensive flows of information required to perform "due diligence" and monitor the performance of borrowers, renders this a more intense form of cooperation than simple information coordination.

The relative gains for individual countries are twofold: first, they gain access to the group's pool of liquid funds and, thus, can economize on their own reserve accumulation; second, as a member of the group, each country gains some influence over the policies of others. The corresponding costs, of course, are that countries must make their own resources available to others, and that access to the group's resource pool comes with conditions attached that may force countries to alter their policies.

Resource coordination has an obvious connection with the motivations for increased economic cooperation in Asia—i.e., it is intended to address the problem of inadequate liquidity support. Indeed, the proposal for an Asian Monetary Fund (AMF) that was floated by the Japanese Government in the midst of the crisis involved precisely this type of mechanism.

Exchange rate coordination

Resource coordination does not presuppose the explicit coordination of exchange rates among member countries. Indeed, IMF as it has been structured since the 1978 Jamaica Agreement involves resource pooling under conditions in which individual member countries are free to choose their own exchange rate regimes. The strongest form of macroeconomic coordination is one in which tight constraints are imposed on the exchange rate and monetary and fiscal policies chosen by individual countries. The more tightly policy choices are constrained, the stronger this third form of coordination becomes. Lying at the extreme, short of political integration, is full monetary unification supplemented by various mechanisms for constraining the choices that individual countries can make in the areas of fiscal and structural policies. The obvious example of such an arrangement is the European Monetary Union.

Exchange rate coordination is a more intense form of coordination than mere resource pooling because resource pooling arrangements are typically required to implement exchange rate coordination while, as noted above, the converse is not true. Exchange rate coordination constrains member country policies more severely. The reasons are as follows.

(i) Under resource pooling, each country retains the discretion to manage its affairs as it sees fit so long as it has no need to draw on the group's resources. Surplus countries that have no need to draw on the group's common resources would not be subjected to loan conditionality. Thus, policy constraints may not be binding on all participating countries.

(ii) Under exchange rate coordination, not only are the policies of *all* member countries constrained, but they are *always* constrained. Participating countries are not free to choose their own exchange rate policies.

(iii) Since coordinated exchange rate policies imply coordinated behavior of one nominal variable in the economy, coordination in the behavior of all other nominal variables is implied as well. In particular, tying exchange rates together means tying money supply growth rates and inflation rates, at least on average and in the long run.

(iv) This last factor has implications for the fiscal policies of participating countries, since it means that each country loses discretion over the amount of seigniorage revenue that it can hope to capture while participating in such an arrangement.

Once again, it is clear how this type of coordination responds to the needs that have been articulated since the Asian crisis. Coordination of exchange rate policy would control the spillovers that have been perceived to arise from exchange rate movements within the region. In particular, it would eliminate the transmission of shocks through changes in competitiveness induced by shifts in relative currency values within the region.

This, then, covers the menu of choices that are now on the table in Asia. The key question that has to be addressed in laying out a road map for improved monetary and financial coordination is how far should Asian countries go down this road? In other words, how much coordination on macroeconomic policies do Asian countries really want, and how much are they individually willing to give up to achieve it?

The next three sections evaluate each of the stops along the road to enhanced coordination on macroeconomic policies. In doing so, the procedure followed is to begin from the weakest forms of coordination and to investigate whether, on the assumption that stronger forms of coordination are not implemented, there is a case for *at least* employing the form of coordination under consideration. Thus, information coordination is taken up first, followed by resource coordination, and then exchange rate coordination. As indicated at the outset, coordination of financial sector reform and development is addressed later in a separate section.

Information exchange

Since sharing already-existing information imposes little cost, the improved sharing of economic information would seem to be a worthwhile goal as long as such information is useful to the recipient. Eichengreen (volume 2), for example, argues that the *general* tendency for contagion to be regional makes a strong case for regional information-sharing and macroeconomic monitoring, not just in Asia, but presumably in other parts of the world as well.

In Asia's case, information about macroeconomic and financial sector developments seems to satisfy the criterion of usefulness to the recipient for at least two reasons.

(i) As emphasized in the core study by Girardin (this volume), similarities in economic and financial structures, as well as in macroeconomic policy regimes, suggest that countries can usefully learn from each other's experiences—i.e., Asia is particularly likely to be characterized by *information* spillovers on macroeconomic issues.

(ii) Regional interdependencies in trade are increasing rapidly, signifying that macroeconomic and financial sector policies can be expected to have progressively larger *economic* spillovers within the region.[4] This makes information about other countries' activities increasingly valuable in formulating domestic policies.

So the indications are that Asian countries would find information about the conditions and policy intentions of their neighbors valuable. This leaves two questions to be addressed, however. The first concerns how sharing information (monitoring) should be conducted, and the second concerns the issue of precisely what is to be done by receiving countries with the information generated. These questions are both critical for the future of monetary and financial cooperation in Asia.

Value added in regional monitoring

The first issue that needs to be addressed is the value of independent regional monitoring over and above what is already carried out by international financial institutions. Regional monitoring complements the existing economic surveillance systems, which were designed when capital was less mobile across countries, in a number of ways. First, it recognizes the complex links that are now being forged among neighboring countries, and provides a

[4] Lee et al (volume 2), for example, show that increases in the share of interregional trade in total trade are empirically associated with a larger importance of region-specific shocks to output, compared with global or country-specific shocks, in a sample of European countries.

mechanism for collaboration and mutually beneficial exchange of experiences. Second, it extends beyond macroeconomic fundamentals into sector and institutional, including social sector, policies. This is because good macroeconomic fundamentals alone no longer provide a guarantee that a country will escape economic difficulties. Monitoring at the regional level alerts policymakers to vulnerabilities that could cause serious economic downturns, and it strengthens their capacity for adjustment. More generally, it allows a group of countries to find their own responses to emerging challenges.

Additional arguments for independent regional monitoring can be based on information advantages, the benefits of specialization, or the value added to information when the producer and user of the information share a common analytical framework.

Because of information advantages that are not readily shared with others outside the region, internal economic expertise may be capable of providing more accurate analysis of macroeconomic conditions than is available to global international financial organizations. It is at least conceivable, for example, that Asian countries may be more willing to engage in a frank exchange of information with a regional monitoring unit over which they exercise substantial direct control than with a global organization where they may exert relatively less influence.

Moreover, a specialized regional monitor may be able to process such information more efficiently than a global monitor. Specifically, it may be able to take advantage of economies of scale and scope in processing information that are not available to a global institution, because of the latter's need to acquire expertise that is worldwide in scope. Indeed, the international community has acknowledged the benefits of regional specialization in processing information in other arenas. These include, for example, the broader area of economic development, where regional development banks play important roles.

Last, countries within Asia may simply find it useful to pass information about each other's economies through a different analytical filter than that of global financial organizations. Regional differences in analytical perspectives and in the diagnosis of international economic problems have always been important. In the past, for example, such differences among the larger industrial countries have proven to be obstacles to negotiations over international monetary reform, as well as to the international coordination of macroeconomic policies. More recently, such differences have also existed at the regional level among western Europe, North America, and Japan. Thus, as a general proposition, there would be nothing unusual in Asia as a region having perspectives and diagnoses of its own macroeconomic problems that may be widely shared within the region, but distinct from those outside. Indeed, the special character of the Asian economic "miracle" already suggested such distinctiveness in approach to the region's economic policies, and the crisis may simply have crystallized the differences. Because a regional monitoring mechanism would provide a device for analyzing macroeconomic developments on the basis of an analytical perspective that Asian countries find congenial, the credibility and perceived usefulness of this information may be raised.

In short, there are potential information advantages as well as benefits of specialization for passing information on the region's macroeconomic conditions through an Asian monitoring mechanism that is separate from global international financial institutions.

Countries already receive information from reports prepared by IMF staff. These are made available to authorities of member countries through their Executive Directors at IMF. Complementing these global-level arrangements, regional-level initiatives at economic monitoring have been undertaken in the postcrisis years. They include setting up the Regional Economic Monitoring Unit (REMU) in ADB. Going forward, therefore, the operative question is not whether a regional monitoring unit should be created, but rather whether present resources should be augmented and, if so, what form should the unit take.

The answers to these questions depend in part on the additional forms of macroeconomic and financial cooperation that turn out to be desirable within the region. Other forms of cooperation (e.g., reserve pooling or exchange rate coordination) may create a case for significantly expanding the role of an independent monitoring unit.

But the answers also depend on a frank assessment of accumulated experience with an independent regional monitoring capacity in Asia. With respect to information coordination, therefore, *the most urgent task facing regional policymakers in the short run is to commit enough resources to the development of an independent regional monitoring capacity. This should allow a fair determination at some point (say in the next 2–3 years) of the extent to which such a capacity can indeed add value to the analysis of Asian macroeconomic developments conducted by global international financial institutions.*

Regional surveillance

The second question posed above is what should be done with the information collected by a regional monitoring unit after it has been filtered by the appropriate regional experts. In other words, should Asian countries move from information coordination to surveillance? Again, this is a critical question for monetary and financial cooperation within Asia. Effective surveillance requires the willingness to surrender some degree of sovereignty over macroeconomic policies as well as to exercise pressure on other countries to modify their policies. Unless Asian countries are capable of committing themselves to an effective peer review (surveillance) process, more intense forms of macroeconomic coordination—which require greater surrender of sovereignty and a greater disposition to intervene in the affairs of others—are likely to prove impractical.

The case for surveillance would seem to be a strong one, particularly if regional "peer pressure" is based on an independent and credible diagnosis of macroeconomic problems. The close economic, political, and cultural ties that exist within Asia give countries a strong incentive to exert pressure on those pursuing undesirable policies. At the same time, these links potentially make this pressure more effective than any that can be exercised by the global community, since regional neighbors may have many more sanctions at their disposal (Girardin, this volume). As long as it is based on an appropriate diagnosis of macroeconomic problems, such discipline can in principle be beneficial to both those exerting the discipline and the country that is subject to it. Thus, there is a strong case for coordination within Asia to be extended beyond mere information exchange to the level of regional surveillance.

For such surveillance to have an impact on policy, however, a forum is required for the reciprocal exchange of views. Again, regional mechanisms have already been devised for carrying out this role, including the Manila Framework Group (MFG), the ASEAN Surveillance Process (ASP), and the ASEAN+3 Economic Review and Policy Dialogue Process. The question is whether these existing mechanisms are suitable for carrying out effective independent regional surveillance.

Wang and Woo (volume 2) have emphasized that if peer pressure is to be effective in forums such as these, their design has to meet specific criteria. In particular, the views expressed during the surveillance process should address clear and observable policy parameters, and the policy recommendations issued by the surveillance forum should be made public. This would harness market reinforcement for peer pressure. These authors have also evaluated existing surveillance initiatives in the Asian region according to these standards. Their findings, in brief, follow.

THE MANILA FRAMEWORK GROUP

While the MFG is seen by some as the leading forum for regional surveillance, Wang and Woo (volume 2) find it wanting. They cite that its membership extends beyond the region and it does not cover all of ASEAN+3; it has not clearly specified the objectives of information exchange and surveillance, and its peer review process is weak.

THE ASEAN SURVEILLANCE PROCESS AND THE ASEAN+3 ECONOMIC REVIEW AND POLICY DIALOGUE PROCESS

The ASP, established in October 1998, is intended to monitor macroeconomic variables, as well as sectoral and social progress. Its peer review process is based on discussions of the surveillance report prepared by the ASEAN Secretariat with inputs from ADB's REMU. Subsequently, the People's Republic of China (PRC),

Japan, and Republic of Korea (Korea) joined ASEAN leaders in discussing economic cooperation in the region. The ASEAN+3 Finance Ministers' Process was established in November 1999. Subsequently the ministers and their deputies initiated their semiannual Economic Review and Policy Dialogue Process and the first ASEAN+3 Finance Ministers meeting was held in May 2000. These are welcome initiatives. However, according to Wang and Woo (volume 2), the region's current surveillance needs to be strengthened significantly. In view of this section's evaluation of the constructive role that regional surveillance can play in Asia, there would be a strong argument for stepping up the effectiveness of the surveillance process even in the absence of more intense forms of regional macroeconomic cooperation. *What is required is a regular and mandatory surveillance process based on specific and clearly identified information provided to a regional policy dialogue whose report to a forum of senior policymakers from the region should cover a broad range of observable policies. This forum should meet regularly to discuss country reports and evaluate country policies, and eventually its key recommendations should be made public.*

A willingness to engage in an enhanced form of mutual surveillance such as this, despite the strong tradition of mutual noninterference in each other's affairs, is the bare minimum required for meaningful monetary and financial cooperation in Asia. The fact that existing surveillance mechanisms do not yet demonstrate such willingness suggests that macroeconomic cooperation within the region remains embryonic.

Resource coordination

With the Chiang Mai Initiative (CMI) in May 2000, macroeconomic cooperation within Asia has in fact already proceeded beyond mere information exchange and surveillance toward some degree of resource coordination. The next step, then, is to evaluate progress and to consider the case for ultimately moving to an even more ambitious level of cooperation. As in the previous section, I will consider the case for resource coordination on its own merits—i.e., even in the absence of more intense coordination in the form of regional exchange rate arrangements.

The case for resource coordination in Asia

The liquid resources required for foreign exchange market intervention may be either owned—in the form of a country's foreign exchange reserves—or borrowed, typically from a global public institution such as IMF. Since the crisis, Asian countries have individually accumulated massive foreign exchange reserves themselves. Doing so is costly because the opportunity cost of assets tied up as foreign exchange reserves is probably much larger than interest earnings on reserves. But individual countries in the region have nonetheless found it desirable to bear these costs, presumably because of dissatisfaction with the alternative global source of liquidity available to them during crises (i.e., the speed of disbursement and scale of IMF lending, as well as the conditions attached).

In view of this, a regional reserve pool administered by Asian countries may offer important advantages over owned reserves as well as global sources of liquid resources. Relative to a country's own reserves, coordination of regional reserve stocks offers the usual insurance advantages of pooling in the face of uncorrelated shocks, thus permitting individual countries to hold smaller amounts of reserves. Relative to global sources of liquidity, regional reserve pooling may also possess an important advantage, in that pooled reserve stocks that are administered at the regional—rather than global—level have the potential to improve the quality of the monitoring associated with the international provision of liquidity. As argued in the last section, neighboring countries may be better placed than a global entity to design and enforce the conditions that must be associated with international liquidity provision to avoid moral hazard.

The advantages of reserve pooling may seem to be self-evident. So one might regard the only relevant questions to be how large the common reserve pool should be and how it should be administered. However, skeptics have questioned both the desirability as well as the feasibility of meaningful reserve-pooling arrangements in the region. Their objections, as outlined below, need to be addressed before proposals for enhancing reserve-pooling mechanisms in the region can be considered.

(i) **Finite resources.** Outside the special set of circumstances in which an Asian Monetary Unit (AMU) would be created—with regional currencies fixed against each other but allowed to float against other currencies—reserve pooling would be used to defend parities against currencies that are outside the pooling arrangement. This means that the stock of reserves available for participating countries to draw on must of necessity be finite. Some observers (e.g., Wyplosz, volume 2) have questioned whether *any* finite stock of reserves can be successful in safeguarding currency values in light of the massive financial resources that are available to market speculators.

(ii) **Spreading contagion.** A second objection is that reserve pooling may itself provide the mechanism for spreading contagion, by compromising the reserves of the strong-currency members of the pooling arrangement when a weak-currency country is attacked and chooses to draw on the arrangement (see Eichengreen 2001).

(iii) **Strong-currency country opt-outs.** Eichengreen has also questioned whether strong-currency countries in the region would actually be willing to support weak-currency ones, pointing to the existence of opt-out clauses within the CMI, and to the fact that even under the European Monetary System (EMS), Germany availed itself of an opt-out clause. This objection would apply even under an AMU-type arrangement to stabilize intraregional exchange rates.

(iv) **Weak conditionality.** Last, some observers have suggested that, in view of Asia's established principle of mutual non-interference and tradition of consensus and informality, the conditionality associated with disbursements out of a pooled stock of reserves would tend to be too weak.

The question is whether these objections vitiate the case for enhanced pooling of reserves in Asia. The answer is probably no. Below, the merits of each of these objections are evaluated.

First, it is undoubtedly true that access to unlimited borrowed reserves makes it more likely that a country would be able to resist a speculative attack on its currency than if it possessed only a limited reserve stock with no access to borrowed reserves. But it surely does not follow that currency values can be sustained only when reserve stocks are in principle infinite. Indeed, theories of speculative attacks that exhibit multiple equilibria typically suggest that there is a range of fundamentals that makes a successful speculative attack possible, and that increases in a country's access to liquid reserves tend to shrink that range. Thus, a larger access to reserves diminishes the probability of a crisis. Reserve adequacy is not an all-or-nothing proposition.

Second, it is true that committing reserves to a pooling arrangement would reduce the stock of reserves that strong-currency countries have available. But the same reasoning as just outlined suggests that, as long as this diminution in its reserve stock does not push such a strong-currency country into the vulnerable range of its fundamentals (i.e., does not make it a weak-currency country), there is no reason to expect reserve pooling to promote the spread of crisis from weak- to strong-currency countries.

The third objection may have more merit, but one might ask why a strong-currency country within the arrangement might indeed be unwilling to support weak-currency ones. One possibility is that if it is required to print its own currency to do so (e.g., Germany within the exchange rate mechanism [ERM]), it may fear inflationary consequences for itself of providing the requisite support. But this objection may lose its force if the currency being provided is that of a third country, as would be true in the absence of an ERM-type of arrangement in which reserve pooling is intended to defend relative currency values among participating countries only, rather than against a third currency such as the US dollar. The second reason that a strong-currency country might be reluctant to extend assistance is out of fear of not being repaid. But this can surely be addressed through the design of appropriate conditionality, which is the mechanism relied upon by IMF to protect the interests of the creditor countries. There is no reason to believe that strong-currency countries within

Asia would be more reluctant to safeguard their own interests in the context of an Asian reserve-pooling arrangement than strong-currency countries outside the region in the context of IMF. This is particularly so since the regional nature of any Asian reserve-pooling arrangement would give such countries a greater voice in the design of the policy conditions intended to ensure repayment.

Evaluation of the last objection depends on what is meant by "weak" conditionality. If it simply means that the conditions attached to lending out of the reserve pool would fail to create adequate safeguards for repayment of the borrowed funds (which seems to assume that lending countries are more indifferent to being repaid than is likely to be the case), then the response is that this cannot be a permanent problem: the pool would be self-liquidating. If instead it means that the conditionality attached, while sufficient to ensure repayment, would nonetheless be different from that required by IMF, then this would presumably be of concern only if such conditionality countenanced the adoption of policies destructive to international prosperity, which would explain the rejection of such conditionality by IMF. But it is hard to imagine that this could be the case, since the close regional economic links that would motivate the adoption of a regional resource-sharing arrangement in the first place would ensure that the participating countries would bear the brunt of such policies. They could therefore be relied upon to be as vigilant about such measures in the design of regional conditionality as is the international community at large in the design of IMF conditionality.

The Chiang Mai Initiative

Overall, the case for enhanced regional resource coordination appears to be a strong one. The remaining questions are how large the pooled resources should be and how they should be administered.

The CMI, agreed upon by the ASEAN+3 in May 2000, represents one set of answers to these questions. Under this initiative, the previously existing ASA within ASEAN was increased to

$1 billion, and a framework for creating a network of bilateral swaps and repurchase agreements between PRC, Japan, and Korea, and individual members of ASEAN was agreed upon (see Appendix 1.1). However, the total amount of resources available under this agreement, amounting to $31.5 billion, is relatively small. It barely exceeds the $17.2 billion that Thailand alone requested from IMF during the crisis. Only a limited number of bilateral arrangements have been agreed upon to date, and the activation of each swap is by mutual agreement between the contracting parties, which essentially implies that it is at the discretion of the country that would provide the hard currency in each case.

Though this arrangement represents a move in the direction of resource coordination, it has some important limitations. First, as already mentioned, the amount of resources available under the CMI is relatively small. At present, for example, if Thailand were to draw on all resources available to it under the CMI, the total amount involved would be about $7 billion. This is substantially below the sum provided by IMF during the crisis, an amount that was perceived as inadequate at the time. Second, since the creation of swap lines is left to bilateral negotiations, it is not clear that all of the members of ASEAN will eventually be able to benefit fully from the agreement. Third, only the first 10% of the amounts available under the bilateral swaps can be drawn upon by a country without an active program with IMF. The remaining 90% is thus essentially subject to IMF conditionality, which fails to address one of the key sources of dissatisfaction within the region with existing global liquidity arrangements. Last, if they are ever needed, activating the swaps may prove to be problematic. Since regional financial stability is a public good, potential creditors in the bilateral swap arrangements may be discouraged from agreeing to activating swap lines by free rider problems.

The implication is that *an adequate arrangement for regional reserve pooling requires extending the CMI into a centralized, multilaterally administered arrangement with substantially larger stocks of resources than are presently available and with the availability of resources increasingly independent of an arrangement with IMF.*

Centralized, multilaterally administered resource pooling would widen access to the resource pool by ASEAN countries (since losses in the event of default would be borne by the group as a whole, rather than by individual creditor countries). This would take advantage of scale economies in dealing with adverse selection and moral hazard problems, and would resolve potential free rider problems that may impair the activation of swap lines under current arrangements.

The decision to create a centralized reserve pool would, of course, need to be accompanied by decisions concerning the magnitude and terms of access. Incorporated into the design, there would also have to be mechanisms for performing due diligence on potential borrowers, designing conditionality, and monitoring performance.

Determining how large the regional reserve pool should be presents a particularly difficult problem. This is both because economic theory provides little guidance regarding the size of the liquid resources that countries may need to be able to call upon to protect themselves from liquidity crises as well as the existence of multiple sources of liquid funds.

In particular, in addition to a regional pool, Asian countries can also draw on their own as well as global sources of liquidity. The potential interactions between regional and global sources of liquidity add a layer of complexity to the problem of determining the appropriate size of the reserve pool. Specifically, it is likely that the availability of an Asian reserve pool would tend to affect the scale of resources made available to participating countries in times of need by IMF. Since IMF lends on the basis of its perception of a country's "balance-of-payments need," the more resources a country can mobilize independently of IMF, the smaller the volume of resources that is likely to be forthcoming from IMF itself. While the degree of "additionality" associated with regionally pooled resources is thus not likely to be one-for-one, it is also not likely to be zero—that is, resources drawn from a regional pool are likely to increase the total amount of liquidity available to countries that enter into an arrangement with IMF. Nonetheless, these interaction effects suggest that *to have a meaningful effect, the resources from the Asian resource pool may need to be comparable in size to those available from IMF.*

The simplest approach to safeguarding the interests of creditors would be to continue to make the availability of resources largely conditional on maintaining an active program with IMF, as is now the case under the CMI. Doing so may indeed have the advantage of allowing the reserve pool to be smaller, since an explicit link to IMF conditionality is likely to increase the "additionality" of regional resources relative to those of IMF. Obviously, however, this does not deal with the appropriateness of conditionality. A natural alternative is to entrust the design of new modalities of conditionality to an independent regional secretariat, which would also absorb the surveillance functions discussed in the last section. However, building up a credible regional surveillance and enforcement capacity is likely to take time. *The timing of the activation of a regional resource pool would thus be determined by that required to accumulate the requisite expertise within a regional secretariat to conduct due diligence on potential borrowers from the pool, to design appropriate conditionality, and to monitor performance.*

Exchange rate coordination

Exchange rate coordination is one aspect of general macroeconomic policy coordination. The relationship between exchange rate coordination and macroeconomic policy coordination more broadly is asymmetric: general macroeconomic policy coordination can be justified in the absence of explicit exchange rate coordination, because macroeconomic spillovers can exist among countries that do not coordinate their exchange rate policies (e.g., the G-8 process). However, exchange rate coordination typically requires coordination in other macroeconomic policies such as monetary and fiscal policies.

From the perspective of an individual country, policy coordination has both benefits and costs. The benefits are that through an explicit mechanism for coordination, a country may be able to exert influence on actions of other countries that may have important effects on the first country. The cost is, of course, that when other countries exercise the same prerogative, the first country may be constrained from acting in ways that it perceives to be in its best interests. Since exchange rate coordination implies other forms of macroeconomic cooperation—specifically with regard to monetary and fiscal policies—the key issue in evaluating its desirability is the trade-off between the benefits and costs of exchange rate, as well as of broader macroeconomic cooperation.

In light of the European experience, an important consideration is whether the ultimate goals of policy coordination in Asia are wholly economic or also partly political. The goal could be political if greater policy coordination is intended to foster increased regional economic integration so that

(i) potential regional political conflicts can be defused—an important assumption driving European integration was that enhanced economic interdependence would induce European countries to focus on common interests; and
(ii) the region can speak with one voice in international affairs—this was also an important motive in Europe, and has played a role in other regional integration initiatives (e.g., the MERCOSUR free trade area in Latin America). As the world economy becomes increasingly globalized and international negotiations on financial and commercial issues intensify, its importance may be increasing over time.

Political goals of this type are important because individual countries in Asia may be willing to sacrifice more of their policy sovereignty and, thus, make coordination more successful, if these goals are important to them.

Motives for exchange rate coordination

However, political goals do *not* indeed appear to be driving suggestions for exchange rate coordination in Asia—or at least, if they are, they appear to be a much weaker source of motivation behind the push for regional economic integration than they were in western Europe. In Europe, political goals were paramount and were perceived as being furthered by enhanced economic integration (though integration was also valued for its own sake, particularly among the smaller economies). In turn, exchange rate coordination was sought to promote economic integration. Thus, exchange rate coordination represented a means for achieving wider and more highly valued ends.

By contrast, the motives for exchange rate coordination in Asia have been quite different. There are motives for pegging exchange rates and motives for doing so in a coordinated fashion.

THE CASE FOR PEGGING

The key motivation underlying the desire for pegged exchange rate arrangements is the perception that floating exchange rates are not compatible with the region's long-established and successful growth strategy. The successful economies in the region have been very open, with development strategies based on trade promotion. These countries have sought to stabilize real exchange rates to promote trade, based on the view that real exchange rate instability discourages trade by creating uncertainty.

However, there are several problems with this argument. The first is that the interpretation of the role of exchange rate policy in the Asian "miracle" experience is open to question. Specifically, by comparison with other developing countries, the Asian "miracle" economies avoided *both* real exchange rate volatility and real exchange rate overvaluation. It is unclear which of these components of exchange rate policy in the region—if either of them—made the most important contribution to the successful growth performance of these countries. This issue is relevant here, since it is possible to conceive of exchange rate arrangements that would incorporate one of these characteristics, but not the other.[5]

Second, while there is increasing evidence that exchange rate instability may indeed have harmful effects on trade, to date the estimated magnitude of this effect tends to be very small (see

[5] For example, "basket, band and crawl" arrangements as advocated by Williamson (2001) could be designed to adjust the central parity so as to avoid persistent overvaluation, while accommodating a substantial amount of short-run nominal (and real) exchange rate instability.

Eichengreen, volume 2). The exceptions to this conclusion have been a number of papers by Rose and others (e.g., Frankel and Rose 2002) that have found large impacts on trade of currency unification. But these studies provide no evidence that the relationship between currency stability and trade is continuous. The effects that they have identified have been associated only with the extreme of sharing a common currency, not with exchange rate stability per se. Moreover, some results of these studies have recently been called into question. In particular, the large measured effects of currency unions on trade may arise from endogeneity bias—i.e., countries that either do, or have the potential to, engage in substantial bilateral trade may be particularly prone to forming currency unions. If so, causation would flow from trade to currency union, rather than vice versa. Indeed, in a recent study by Tenreyro (2002), the large currency union effect on trade shows up when bilateral trade equations are estimated by ordinary least square (OLS), but becomes statistically insignificant under an instrumental variable technique that attempts to isolate the independent effect of common currencies on trade.

Last, even if the interpretation of the Asian experience as described is correct, it may suggest that what matters, and therefore what should be sought, is exchange rate stability relative to markets outside the region, rather than among regional economies. This would be consistent with the emergence of an East Asian "dollar zone" prior to the crisis.

THE CASE FOR COORDINATING

The motivation for exchange rate coordination, on the other hand, does directly concern exchange rate stability within the region. It is based on spillover effects associated with relative exchange rate movements among regional currencies, and draws its impetus in part from alternative interpretations of how contagion spread among Asian countries during the 1997 financial crisis.

One interpretation is that contagion during the crisis reflected a "wake-up call" effect, issued to investors by large exchange rate movements. According to this view, therefore, limiting large movements of exchange rates would tend to limit the scope for contagion.

Unfortunately, the "wake-up call" mechanism is only one of many ways that contagion may have been spread during the crisis, and there is no professional consensus on what the precise channels of contagion were. Further, even to the extent that "wake-up call" contagion was important, it is by no means obvious that it was necessarily transmitted through exchange rate movements. Sharp movements in exchange rates were only one component of the crisis, which also featured massive bankruptcies, the collapse of asset prices, and acute output contractions.

It is possible to argue that all these accompanying phenomena were themselves caused by exchange rate movements, but even if this was so, there is no particular reason to believe that sharp swings in exchange rates would have similar effects in the region in the future. After all, the international experience does not suggest that sharp exchange rate movements are invariably associated with economic collapses. More generally, it is not clear that in the future, markets will tend to regard sharp exchange rate movements in one Asian country as being informative about the value of assets in other countries in the region. The special circumstances that linked many of these countries in the past, including similarities in regional development models, financial fundamentals, and market perceptions of the creditworthiness of the "miracle" economies, are unlikely to prevail. Moreover, markets may have learned from the recent international crisis experience. As a result of that learning, as well as of the improved information flows that these crises have brought about, they may have become much more discriminating than they were in 1997.

The second justification for seeking exchange rate stability within the region interprets contagion as having spread from country to country during the Asian crisis through trade channels, as the result of competitive devaluations. As mentioned previously, competitive devaluations can be interpreted analytically as a process through which countries reach a noncooperative Nash equilibrium. All the participating parties are worse off (because all countries experience exchange rate instability and undergo an increase in their domestic price levels, but none of them gains a competitive advantage relative to their commercial rivals) than they could be if they were able to coordinate their actions. Thus, exchange rate coordination is required to move all countries to the superior cooperative equilibrium.[6]

The empirical question is whether Asian countries actually perceive a payoff structure that would induce them to behave in the manner assumed by the competitive devaluation perspective in the absence of coordination. Precrisis experience in the region would seem to suggest that they do not since, left to their own devices, most of the crisis countries adopted a de facto US dollar peg that revealed a preference for exchange rate stability as opposed to seeking competitive advantage. Indeed, the insistence of these countries in adhering to these dollar pegs in the face of the loss of competitiveness in the context of US dollar appreciation has been cited by many observers as an important factor in the crisis. Postcrisis, the adherence of the PRC and Hong Kong, China to their currency pegs in the face of massive devaluations by their competitors, and the Malaysian strategy of adopting a fixed rate (at a level that was *appreciated* relative to its pre-fixing level) also suggest that the fear of competitive devaluation can be exaggerated.

On the other hand, the crisis also suggests that this fear has some basis in fact. Indonesia, for example, floated its currency before it had been heavily attacked, and the currency movements in the fall of 1997 in Singapore and Taipei,China—two economies with strong financial fundamentals compared with the crisis countries—may have owed something to a competitive devaluation effect. Similarly, with the exception of Malaysia, postcrisis exchange rate policies in the crisis countries at least leave room for the possibility that competitiveness concerns may have been in the forefront of the minds of policymakers. All these economies resisted a too-rapid appreciation of their real exchange rates after the initial overshooting associated with the crisis.[7]

---

[6] As mentioned in the introduction, some adherents of this view interpret contagion as having spread during the Asian crisis not through a "wake-up call" mechanism, but through trade channels.

[7] See Hernandez and Montiel (2002). Of course, a "concern with competitiveness" is not the same thing as a competitive devaluation, since that concern need not have been driven by the behavior of other countries in the region.

Skeptics of the competitive devaluation view (Eichengreen 2001) maintain that the competitive devaluation concern is weakened by the fact that trade within the region is small. But it is not so small and is growing. In any case, competitiveness in third markets may play just as important a role in driving competitive devaluations as trade within the region. Overall, then, of the two arguments adduced for the desirability of regional exchange rate coordination, this one seems more persuasive.

Proposals for exchange rate coordination

Leaving aside the merits of the general case for currency coordination within Asia, consider next how such coordination could be brought about. Specific proposals follow.

(i) Create an "Asian currency unit" (ACU) that ties Asian currency values to each other while allowing the ACU to float against the rest of the world, in the manner of the former European currency unit.

This form of coordination is alleged to have the virtues not only of preventing competitive devaluations—i.e., of providing the institutional means of moving the countries in the region to a cooperative equilibrium—but of doing so while providing resources that are (at least in principle) unlimited in support of relative regional exchange rate parities. At the same time, it allows the artificial regional currency to adjust in response to shocks that are specific to the region but asymmetric with respect to those affecting the rest of the world (see Wyplosz, volume 2).

(ii) Adopt a joint basket peg, in which all participating countries define their exchange rate policies with reference to a common currency basket. At one extreme, the countries could all peg to that basket. Alternatively, they could operate different types of bands around the common basket.

Ogawa et al (volume 2) advocated the pegged version of this arrangement. It would provide not only intra-regional exchange rate stability, but also exchange rate stability relative to trading partners outside the region. The more flexible "band" version, suggested by Frankel (volume 2), attempts to strike a balance between the desire to avoid the noncooperative equilibrium while allowing individual countries substantial discretion over their particular regime choices.

(iii) Adopt an *explicit* common peg to a single currency, such as the yen or the US dollar.

The dollar version of such an arrangement, proposed by McKinnon (volume 2), is advocated for transparency. Also, it stabilizes bilateral exchange rates against all major competitors and trading partners; provides an effective nominal anchor for the domestic price level; and anchors long-run exchange rate expectations, thus providing incentives for stabilizing speculation (based on regressive expectations), as well as for developing long-term domestic financial instruments.

These options face problems, however. Some are specific to a coordinating mechanism, while others apply to all of them. The specific ones are as follows.

(i) **An Asian currency unit.** The ACU proposal faces the problem that (unlike Europe) Asia as a whole is *not* relatively closed. Also (as in Europe), unlimited support for weak-currency countries may be hard to extract from strong-currency countries, while (unlike Europe) Asia would have to employ such a system in the context of capital accounts that are already quite open.

While regional trade is indeed large and growing in Asia, this is partly due to the openness of these economies. This suggests that exchange rate stability vis-à-vis the outside world would compete as an objective with exchange rate stability within the region—i.e., preferences in favor of regional arrangements are likely to be less strong than they were in Europe.

(ii) **Joint basket pegs.** In principle, this key flaw of the ACU is addressed by proposals for a joint basket peg. This would tend to stabilize intraregional exchange rates (as long as it included most countries in the region) as well as exchange rates against trading partners outside the region. However, the joint basket peg proposal faces the problems of inducing countries to adhere to a basket that may be individually suboptimal for each of them, as well as of devising currency weights that optimally take into account current and capital account transactions. In its "pegged" version, it faces the difficulty of providing the resources to defend pegs to which countries may not be strongly committed. In its "flexible" version, it faces the problem of verifiability, while it also may fail to solve the coordination problem.

Skeptics note that, even if each country considered it desirable to operate a fixed exchange rate regime, a common peg is likely to be suboptimal for each individual country. That being the case, adherence to a common peg would involve weighing the benefits of a tailor-made national exchange rate policy against costs associated with the probability of a noncooperative Nash outcome. If the latter is assessed to be small (and as indicated above, the evidence is inconclusive), countries whose optimal national exchange rate policies were far from that implied by the joint peg would be unlikely to subscribe to or eventually adhere to the regime. That would reduce its value for other countries. Thus, the viability of the system would depend on the extent to which optimal national policies are consistent with the common peg. Unfortunately, even when the range of optimal regimes is restricted to pegged rates, with currency weights designed only with the objective of stabilizing trade in goods and services, Ogawa et al (volume 2) find that optimal currency weights tend to differ widely across Asian countries.

But a separate argument against common basket pegs is precisely that the optimal weights for such a peg should *not* be based solely on trade considerations, as is often suggested. Doing so privileges the trade balance relative to capital account transactions, a procedure that has no basis in theory. Once this is acknowledged, it becomes difficult to devise an optimal *national* peg, not to mention a regional one.

That capital account considerations must be factored into the design of an optimal basket peg seems clear because, after all, there is no presumption that exchange rate risk would tend to discourage intratemporal trade more effectively than it does intertemporal trade. Indeed, the reduced perception of exchange rate risk as the result of stable exchange rates relative to the US dollar has been cited as an important factor contributing to large capital inflows in Asian countries before the 1997 financial crisis. Evidence that exchange rate instability has tended to discourage capital flows into Asia is summarized in Ogawa et al (volume 2).[8]

Once the need to factor in capital-account considerations is acknowledged, it becomes difficult to design an optimal peg for an individual country, and even more so an optimal *common* peg for a diverse group of countries with different degrees of access to international capital markets. The very difficulty of devising the optimal peg makes any common peg harder to sustain, because uncertainty about the optimal composition of the peg is likely to weaken governments' adherence to *any* agreed peg, making it more vulnerable to speculative attacks.

(iii) **Single-currency common pegs.** A common peg against the yen suffers from the liability that it is hard to justify on the basis of optimal-currency-area criteria. The alternative that has been suggested for Asia, an explicit common peg to the US dollar, suffers from similar flaws.

For example, Barro (volume 2) notes that Hong Kong, China; Malaysia; and Singapore are the only Asian economies with trade shares in gross domestic product

[8] The authors actually use this evidence to argue in *favor* of a common peg featuring a prominent role for the yen, on the basis of the view that the discouragement of capital inflows to the region before the crisis would have been a *good* thing. However, this argument is not very convincing because (i) future capital inflows may not prove as harmful as precrisis flows if the distortions that caused the latter to have negative effects are removed; (ii) if it is desirable to discourage capital inflows, market-based capital account restrictions can do so without introducing unnecessary uncertainty into trade transactions; and (iii) if it were nonetheless desired to introduce nominal exchange rate uncertainty, this could be done simply by allowing the exchange rate to float.

(GDP) with Japan that are in excess of 20% (Indonesia's share is about 15%). But output and relative price co-movements for Hong Kong, China and Singapore are actually higher with the US than they are with Japan. Indeed, based on trade shares as well as output and price co-movements, he concludes that not only Hong Kong, China and Singapore, but also the Philippines, would be better served by joining a common currency area with the US, rather than with Japan. In the same study, Barro finds that *only* Hong Kong, China; Philippines; and Singapore among Asian economies would be well served by participating in a "dollar area."[9]

Moreover, some advantages claimed for single-currency common pegs appear to be overstated.

(a) Single-currency common pegs would tend to stabilize bilateral exchange rates against all major trading partners only if G-3 exchange rates were also stabilized among themselves.

(b) The advantages of a single-currency common peg in providing a stable nominal anchor for the economy do not carry much weight if countries have independently established their anti-inflationary credentials, as is true of most Asian countries.

(c) While macroeconomic stability may be conducive to financial development, it is not clear that it is a sufficient condition, or that pegging the exchange rate is either necessary or sufficient for establishing macroeconomic stability.

Beyond the flaws just described that are specific to each of the currency coordination proposals, all these proposals share two general flaws that suggest that efforts to coordinate exchange rates must proceed relatively slowly in Asia.

---

[9] Actually, Barro asks a different question: *if* the countries in question were to seek monetary unification with the dollar, yen, or euro, which of the major currencies would be optimal to adopt? But the criteria involved—trade shares and co-movements in relative price and outputs—are the same as would be applied in choosing among single-currency pegs.

(a) **Feasibility.** The first problem is that it is not clear that *any* coordinated pegged exchange rate arrangement would be feasible in Asia under current conditions. This is essentially an application of the fashionable "bipolar" view of exchange rate regimes. This view, though often overstated, contains an important kernel of truth that is relevant to Asia. This is that, when capital mobility is high, the sustainability of an announced exchange rate peg depends on whether perceived benefits to authorities of adhering to the peg are large enough to outweigh the costs of doing so in the face of a speculative attack. The problem in the Asian case is that, unlike in Europe, the "side benefits" of playing by the rules of the currency coordination game may not be evident. Combined with open capital accounts that characterize many countries in Asia, this would make any coordination scheme difficult to sustain.

Unlike Europe, Asia has no preexisting "nexus of contracts" that makes for credible currency commitments, in the sense that the benefits of such contracts for individual countries (e.g., free trade areas or customs unions) would be jeopardized by failure to live up to currency commitments. Also, unlike in Europe, monetary unification in Asia is not supported by an overwhelming commitment to political integration. Given these differences, Asian countries would tend to have weaker incentives to adhere to an exchange rate coordination arrangement that constrains their exchange rate choices than did European countries.

Moreover, in contrast with the European experience, currency coordination in Asia would have to be carried out in the context of already-opened capital markets. Regional trade integration and exchange rate stability came first in Europe, while capital mobility and monetary unification came last. Full capital account liberalization was not achieved until 1990 in western Europe, and the 1992 ERM crisis provides a sobering reminder that when the capital account is open and the benefits of adhering to a regional peg are not perceived as exceeding the cost, the peg becomes impossible to sustain. Indeed, Wyplosz (volume 2) argues that it was capital account liberalization that led to rapid monetary unification in western Europe, since the authorities realized that the ERM could not survive under the open capital accounts that prevailed after the early 1990s. If this was so in Europe, where the benefits of adhering to regional currency arrangements were probably perceived to be much larger than they are likely to be in Asia, that does not bode well for the prospects for Asian currency coordination.

(b) **Optimality.** Any form of currency coordination in Asia would preclude continuing individually floating exchange rates that most of the former crisis countries in the region maintain. A second general objection to exchange rate coordination in the region—at least in the near term—is that there are strong reasons to believe that present exchange rate arrangements may indeed be optimal.

The pattern of exchange rate movements among the crisis countries featured a sharp short-run depreciation, followed by a slow recovery. This was associated with a combination of substantial reserve accumulation and much more volatility than prior to the crisis, except in the case of Malaysia. The accumulation of reserves in these countries suggests that they were actively involved in slowing the pace of recovery from the original crisis-induced exchange rate overshooting. The combination of no formal exchange rate commitment, relatively depreciated real exchange rates, large reserve stocks, and substantial short-run nominal exchange rate volatility would have worked to sustain an export-led recovery of real activity; provide a liquidity cushion against sudden, discrete disruptions of currency values; discourage speculation by removing one-way bets; and discourage the accumulation of unhedged foreign-currency liabilities (see Hernandez and Montiel [2002]). It is precisely this kind of optimal use of exchange rate policy at the individual country level that would be precluded by regional exchange rate coordinating arrangements in the near term.

The upshot is that, with respect to coordination on macroeconomic matters, *for the short term at least, while the road for Asia should include enhanced surveillance and reserve pooling, efforts to promote coordination of exchange rate should proceed on a relatively slower track. The purely economic benefits in the form of forestalling the emergence of a noncooperative competitive devaluation equilibrium do not seem worth the costs at the individual country level of forgoing sovereignty over exchange rate policy. Moreover, if markets come to share this view, the prevalence of open capital markets in the region will make any cooperative arrangement difficult to sustain in the face of shocks that would call for an exchange rate response in the absence of the cooperative arrangement.*

This leaves open the question, however, of regional exchange rate arrangements in the long run. There is clearly no reason to rule out cooperative arrangements on exchange rates—including the possibility of currency unification among the ASEAN+3 countries or some subset of them. Indeed, there are reasons to believe that changes that are taking place within Asia are likely to move countries in such a direction. To see how, recall that coordination on exchange rate policy in the context of high capital mobility requires market perceptions that governments have strong reasons to adhere to their agreed exchange rate pegs. In other words, that the benefits of doing so from the perspective of individual countries exceed the costs. The benefits as well as the costs are likely to evolve over time in a manner that will enhance the feasibility of regional exchange rate arrangements.

On the benefit side, the accelerated pace of development of regional economic institutions and political arrangements since the Asian crisis is likely to be conducive to the gradual emergence of a "web of interrelated contracts" among participating countries. This would enhance the credibility of a regional exchange rate arrangement by giving Asian countries a greater stake in abiding by regional agreements on economic issues. The existence of just such a "web of interrelated contracts" was crucial in creating the perception that European countries had much to gain from adherence to European exchange rate arrangements.

On the cost side, the key cost of abiding by a regional exchange rate arrangement is the forgoing of national autonomy over exchange rate policy. But how significant a loss this represents depends on the value of the exchange rate as an instrument for macroeconomic adjustment. This value, in turn, depends inversely on the extent to which countries in East Asia satisfy the criteria for an optimal currency area. As indicated above, Asian countries probably do not meet these criteria closely enough at present to make it credible that they can afford to eschew occasional nominal exchange rate adjustments. However, this does not preclude better meeting these criteria in the future, thereby reducing the value of the exchange rate as an adjustment instrument. Indeed, recent research suggests that the Asian region may already come close to the Europe of 20 years ago in meeting some economic criteria for an optimal currency area. As trade and financial integration increases within East Asia, it is easy to imagine the region moving in this direction. Specifically, given the relatively flexible labor markets and the substantial intraregional labor mobility, if enhanced integration reduces the incidence of asymmetric shocks, it is possible that the perceived costs of forgoing intraregional exchange rate adjustments will diminish sufficiently to make regional exchange rate coordination feasible.

Thus, the way forward on exchange rates would seem to be an incremental one: to develop stronger cooperative regional institutions and to move regional economic integration forward in other ways, thereby allowing the conditions to develop that may ultimately make regional exchange rate coordination arrangements feasible. The question will then arise whether it will be *optimal* to implement such arrangements.

In short, closer intraregional institutional and economic relationships created through the mechanisms for regional macroeconomic cooperation proposed in this overview study may ultimately pave the way for closer cooperation in exchange rate policy as well. But decisions in this area can and should await future developments.

Coordination on financial sector reform and development

As indicated, it is useful to distinguish between coordination on financial sector issues and on macroeconomic issues. Either of the two can be conducted without the other, which suggests that each type of coordination needs to be independently evaluated on its own merits.

The structural economic agenda for Asia is focused on financial sector and corporate governance reform. There is a strong general case for international coordination on these issues, based on two observations (see Eichengreen [2001]). First, the spillovers associated with financial crises suggest that financial stability is a public good in which individual countries, because they ignore the effects on their neighbors, would tend to underinvest. Second, since capital is likely to flow to countries where financial regulation is more lax, international coordination is also justified by the need to avoid a "race to the bottom" in financial regulation.

Supplementing the general case for international cooperation on these matters is a separate case for even more intense cooperation within the Asian region. That case is based on the following two observations.

(i) The postcrisis diagnosis of financial sector problems shares many common features across Asian countries. All, for example, featured vulnerable bank-based financial systems with a history of a substantial government role in guiding the allocation of resources, and in each of them domestic and external financial deregulation was undertaken without sufficient strengthening of the regulatory and supervisory structure.

(ii) There is no optimal, universally valid, financial structure that should necessarily represent the ultimate goal of reform in Asia. The problems of asymmetric information and opportunistic behavior that characterize financial transactions are universal, and have the effect of making financial intermediation a productive economic activity everywhere. But countries with advanced financial systems exhibit institutional ways of coping with these problems. Cross-country comparisons, for example, reveal important differences in the strength of creditors' rights, in the roles of banks versus securities markets in the allocation of resources, etc. Moreover, there is no consensus over the superiority of one type of financial structure over another (e.g., bank-based versus securities-based) in performing financial functions effectively. These differences suggest that there may be room for "searching and learning" in Asia, with the possibility of developing an "Asian way" of dealing with these problems. This might achieve the same standards of stability and efficiency as those elsewhere, but perhaps in a different manner (e.g., with a different combination of prudential measures).

These considerations suggest that there may be advantages to pooling regional resources in dealing with financial sector reform and development issues, so that each country does not have to reinvent the wheel in what is likely to be a region-specific and idiosyncratic process.

To address this objective, Eichengreen (2001) has proposed creating a specialized regional institution, dubbed the Asian Financial Institute (AFI). This would have the mandate to coordinate financial sector reform and development within Asia. It would do so in part by promoting the exchange of information—i.e., by collecting and disseminating information on regional financial sector reform experiences, providing technical assistance, running training programs, and providing a venue for meetings of regional financial sector experts. It could also engage in other activities, such as providing clearance and settlement functions for participating central banks.

Under Eichengreen's plan, the AFI would have the role of developing common regional prudential measures for finance. Commonality in prudential standards would avoid crisis spillovers and the "race to the bottom" problem described previously, and the AFI would provide a venue for negotiating common agreements on broad guidelines for financial standards. Eichengreen also envisions a role for the institution in enforcing such standards.

However, coordinating in financial sector reform and development and adopting common minimum prudential standards do not have to mean uniformity in structures or standards. Pooling information and expertise on financial reform within the region is called for by the information spillovers described above, while avoiding crisis spillovers and a "race to the bottom" may call for regional guidelines on prudential issues. But these forms of cooperation do not necessarily imply regional uniformity: just as an "Asian way" may develop for financial sector reform and development that shares common features across the region but differs from financial structures and standards elsewhere, diversity on these issues may also arise within the region. While harmonizing standards, legal and regulatory systems, and tax treatment would undoubtedly help cross-border financial flows, this benefit has to be traded off against benefits that may have to be forgone, in the form of opportunities to adapt institutions and standards to local conditions.

The example of Europe is instructive. As emphasized in the core study by Girardin (this volume), financial cooperation in Europe was based on an "open coordination" model that uses emulation for the spread of best practice and relies on trust and self-control, rather than on legally binding commitments. Under this model, countries define common objectives, fix regional guidelines combined with specific timetables for meeting objectives, establish qualitative and quantitative benchmarks against best practice, and translate regional guidelines into national policies by adopting specific policies tailored to national circumstances. Thus, European Union coordination on financial sector reform and development has tended to be flexible and has lacked a supranational dimension. Minimum regional standards for prudential rules, recognizing regional needs, were adopted in the 1980s. Beyond this, however, there was no attempt at further regional harmonization. Instead, countries agreed to mutually recognize each other's regulations and adhere to the subsidiarity principle for supervision policy.

Indeed, beyond the general common features described above, Asian financial systems offer substantial diversity. Accordingly, the more flexible model of cooperation seems best suited to the region. Such a model would seem to address the stake that all countries in the region may have in the adequacy of the prudential framework, while at the same time allowing for institutional flexibility to adapt to local conditions.

Financial cooperation in Asia has barely started. Regional meetings among regulators and supervisors do occur, but infrequently and with no clear agenda or timetable (Girardin, this volume). The next section offers some proposals for stepping up coordination on financial sector development and reform under a flexible "open coordination" model.

Conclusions and recommendations—the road map

There is a relatively strong case for effective regional economic surveillance within Asia, as well as for enhanced regional resource pooling, expanding the CMI in scope, and providing it with its own permanent secretariat. There is also a good case for a joint regional initiative on cooperation in financial sector reform and development. These ideas seem worthy not only on their own merits, but also as fillips to regional institution-building in Asia that could lay the groundwork for additional integration efforts. On the other hand, regional exchange rate coordination, whether in the form of a regional basket peg, an AMU, or full monetary unification, seems premature.

These proposals are consistent with a variety of future institutional arrangements, including the eventual launching of an Asian

Monetary Cooperation Fund (AMCF) in the medium term with responsibilities in three areas:

(i) regional surveillance,
(ii) regional reserve management, and
(iii) guiding and monitoring regional financial development.

The recommendations below entail the creation of a regional policy dialogue unit that would also have an important role in developing and enforcing the conditionality to be associated with drawing on the region's pooled reserves (the first two areas of cooperation identified above). They also require a secretariat charged with providing technical expertise and collecting information on financial sector reform and development. Economies of scale and scope suggest that these should be housed in the same institution.

While constituting a new AMCF to carry out the recommendations provided below would create a major single focal point for future regional monetary and financial integration efforts, the decision is likely to rely on considerations that go beyond the scope of this study. Accordingly, the recommendations address specific needs identified without presupposing the creation of such an institution in the short run.

Regional surveillance

For regional surveillance, an independent, well-funded and staffed regional policy dialogue unit should be established during the next stage of Asian cooperation—i.e., over the next 2 years. This unit should focus, in the short run, on ways that it can add value to the monitoring activities already carried out by global international financial institutions. This may include the development of crisis early-warning systems that rely on regional expertise, as well as planning for independent regionally tailored conditionality to be associated with lending arising from regional pooling of reserves (to be discussed next). From its inception, the new regional policy dialogue unit should represent both an independent warehouse of information on the state of the regional economies and an independent source of analysis of regional economic developments. The unit could be housed in a new AMCF with the responsibilities outlined above, or if an overarching new regional institution is not created in the short run, it could be housed within an existing one. This unit would submit its own regular reports on macroeconomic and financial market conditions in participating countries to a regional surveillance group, which in turn must ultimately be the judge of the added value that an independent regional monitoring unit can provide in Asia. Reports prepared by the policy dialogue unit should contain data on external accounts, monetary and financial accounts, fiscal position, and real sector resilience, as well as on other variables such as poverty rates and political developments, and major institutional and legal changes (Girardin, this volume). Discussions within the surveillance group would focus on well-defined and quantifiable policy areas, and each regular country discussion would conclude by making policy recommendations to the member country. Following Wang and Woo (volume 2), adherence to these recommendations would be encouraged through peer pressure (in part by having each report discuss progress that the country may or may not have made in acting on past recommendations) as well as through market pressures, since the policy recommendations would be made public. This enhanced surveillance process could be undertaken as soon as the unit is capable of preparing the detailed country reports that the process would require.

Regional resource pooling

As indicated earlier, the CMI is quite small relative to the owned reserves of member countries or to the resources to which these countries have access through IMF. It is also largely grafted onto IMF conditionality and administered bilaterally. These characteristics should be reviewed, including the size of the facility. The costly accumulation of reserves by individual Asian countries is continuing apace and no major revamping of the international financial architecture appears to be in the offing that will ameliorate Asian countries' appetite for liquidity protection. Another feature that will have to be reviewed is the bilateral arrangement because it may undermine access to funds from the facility when they are most needed.

In the near term (again, over the next 2 years or so) the ASEAN+3 countries should seek to enlarge the swap lines available under the CMI, with the objective of at least doubling the volume of resources committed. They could also consider earmarking a portion of the foreign exchange reserves for financing short-term liquidity needs of the member countries. Simultaneously, the ASEAN+3 countries should negotiate methods for administering a future regional reserve pool that would replace bilateral swap arrangements in the medium term (say, in 3–5 years). At that time, resources previously committed to bilateral swaps would instead be permanently committed to a central regional reserve fund, and decisions regarding the disbursements of these funds would be made on a multilateral basis. The key subjects for negotiation, of course, would be the formula that would determine each country's contribution to the fund and how decisions concerning disbursements are made. Under a new AMCF, for example, an Executive Board in which voting is weighted according to a country's total contributions to the resources available from the pool could ultimately be entrusted with the responsibility for authorizing the activation of a drawing.

In the short run, disbursements under the CMI should continue to be piggybacked on compliance with IMF program conditions. The development of independent conditionality for the CMI or a more centralized reserve pool is particularly dependent on substantial improvements in the region's independent surveillance capacity. Only when such capacity has been developed and when experience with regional surveillance has been accumulated will it be possible to determine whether the availability of pooled regional resources should continue to be conditioned on policy criteria specified by IMF. It is the need to accumulate such experience at the regional level that precludes the feasibility of activating a centralized regional reserve pool sooner than the medium-term time frame of 3–5 years. As discussed in the core study by Chaipravat (this volume), if independent regional conditionality is ultimately adopted, it may be based on certification of eligibility to draw based on compliance with regional guidelines in macroeconomic performance or financial sector reform (see next topic), as well as on the undertaking of future commitments regarding macroeconomic policies and/or outcomes.

The regional reserve pool could provide the opportunity to explore the feasibility and desirability of regional exchange rate coordination in the medium term. In particular, it would be possible to build incentives for such coordination into any reserve-pooling arrangement. For any such arrangement to add to the liquid resources available to participating countries, they would have to be eligible to draw from the pool some multiple of the resources that they contribute to it. The size of that multiple could be determined by a number of factors. Also, by linking access rights to exchange rate policy, it would be possible to create incentives for exchange rate coordination while leaving countries complete discretion over their exchange rate arrangements.

To do so, a synthetic common "composite peg" could be designed that includes the US dollar, the yen, and the euro. Access rights to the common reserve pool could then be expressed as a multiple of the country's contribution to the pool that would be a (decreasing) function of the extent to which the country's currency deviates from the value implied by the common peg.

Such an arrangement has several virtues.

(i) It would make economic sense, since a country's demand for liquidity should be inversely related to the extent of exchange rate variability that it is willing to countenance. Thus, it would be natural for a country that persistently allows greater exchange rate fluctuations to make smaller drawings from the pool.

(ii) It would also provide an incentive for countries to adhere more closely to the common peg, by penalizing competitive devaluations through a reduction of access to the reserve pool.

(iii) Negotiations on the shape of the function linking the drawing "multiple" to exchange rate deviations from the "shadow" common peg would reveal the extent to which countries truly want to limit exchange rate variability within the region.

Even if regional exchange rate coordination is probably a long-term project, such a mechanism could be introduced at the inception of the centralized regional reserve pool—or at any time after—to lay the groundwork.

Regional cooperation on financial sector reform and development

As argued in this overview study, regional cooperation on financial sector reform and development should proceed simultaneously with cooperation on macroeconomic issues. This is appropriately conducted within the ASEAN+3 group. The specific recommendation is that such cooperation be initiated in three successive, partly overlapping phases.

(i) **Phase 1 (first 2 years).** In this phase, countries would cooperate, through information exchange and a common indicative template, on mechanisms for postcrisis management of the financial sector (e.g., cleaning up balance sheets, closing banks, identifying the roles of asset management corporations, bank mergers, and government ownership).

(ii) **Phase 2 (years 3–5).** The second phase involves cooperation in developing effective mechanisms for regulation and supervision. This involves setting up general regional guidelines for prudential regulation (to be adapted to domestic needs under the principle of mutual recognition) as well as the extension of the supervisory function within each country to all institutions that engage in banking activities. The forum for the regional guidelines as well as for the exchange of information on domestic regulatory and supervisory reform would be an East Asian Banking Advisory Committee (EABAC), comprising high-level representatives of the participating countries' supervisory authorities and finance ministries. The EABAC should meet four times a year. A newly established secretariat would assist in the EABAC's work. During this phase, the secretariat would begin with the development of regional financial stress indicators, complementing the work mentioned above on early warning systems at the macro level by the regional macroeconomic policy dialogue unit. The financial and macroeconomic support units could both be housed in an AMCF.

(iii) **Phase 3 (over 5 years).** The third phase would carry out whatever degree of regional harmonization of regulations is required to eventually permit the full unification of regional financial markets. Harmonization would come only in this third phase because, since it involves detailed international negotiation and agreement, it is much more demanding and time consuming than formulating general regional guidelines for prudential regulation in phase 2. *Establishment of full regional financial liberalization—an East Asian Financial Area*—would require the absence of restrictions on capital movements within the region, the presence of well-functioning regulatory and supervisory mechanisms within each country subject to regional guidelines, and the harmonization of various regional financial regulations. These ingredients would have been put in place during phases 1 and 2 and the initial period of this phase.

The proposals in the preceding three sections comprise a road map for future financial and monetary cooperation in East Asia and are summarized in Table 1.1. Carrying them out would permit the region to grow in a significantly more stable macroeconomic and financial environment than has characterized the recent past.

Table 1.1 **Road Map for Promoting Monetary and Financial Cooperation in East Asia**

	Information Exchange and Surveillance System	Resource Sharing
Short term (within the next 2 years)	Establish an independent regional policy dialogue unit to • Prepare reports to "kick off" peer review meetings. Early Warning System should be an integral part. • Monitor regional financial developments (including adoption and implementation of best practices). • Develop terms of reference and conditionality to be associated with lending from a centralized reserve pool (to be established in the medium term).	Expand the Bilateral Swap Agreement Network under the Chiang Mai Initiative (CMI), and consider earmarking a portion of foreign exchange reserves for financing short-term liquidity needs of member countries.
Medium term (3–5 years)	Develop alternative conditionality for balance-of-payments support.	Replace bilateral swaps under the CMI with a centralized pool that seeks to prevent financial crisis in the region.
Longer term (over 5 years)		

Exchange Rate Coordination	Financial Sector Cooperation
	Cooperate on postcrisis management of the financial sector. Technical assistance should be provided to individual countries where appropriate.
Explore the feasibility of exchange rate coordination by conditioning drawings from the reserve pool on exchange rate policies.	Set up general regional guidelines for prudential regulation, enhancing cooperation on these issues by establishing an East Asian Banking Advisory Committee. Extend the supervisory function within each country to all institutions that engage in banking activities.
If warranted, implement regional exchange rate arrangements to promote stability of intraregional exchange rates. Begin with soft pegging to a basket; then move to hard pegging. Eventually a European Monetary System-type arrangement (which includes Japan) could be considered. The adoption of a common currency would be the last step.	Implement whatever degree of regional harmonization of regulations is required to eventually permit the full unification of regional financial markets. Establish an East Asian Financial Area.

APPENDIX 1.1

Existing arrangements for financial cooperation in Asia

The ASEAN Swap Arrangement

The initial agreement establishing the ASEAN Swap Arrangement (ASA) was signed in Kuala Lumpur in 1977 by the original five Association of Southeast Asian Nations (ASEAN) countries (Indonesia, Malaysia, Philippines, Singapore, and Thailand). It was intended to provide short-term financial support to member countries with balance-of-payments needs through short-term swap facilities. Each member contributed $40 million and was eligible to draw up to twice that amount for periods of 1, 2, or 3 months, with one possible renewal. The facility has been extended several times, but its relatively small size has meant that the level of utilization has been low. From 1979 to 1992, it was used only by Indonesia in 1979, Malaysia and Thailand in 1980, and the Philippines in 1981 and 1992.

The ASEAN Arrangement to Borrow

The ASEAN Arrangement to Borrow (AAB) was established in the mid-1990s. All ASEAN countries participate. Member countries are classified into two groups. Countries in Group 1 (Brunei Darussalam, Indonesia, Malaysia, Philippines, Singapore, and Thailand) contribute $100 million each, while those in Group 2 (Cambodia, Lao People's Democratic Republic [Lao PDR], Myanmar, and Viet Nam) contribute $25 million each. Each member country is eligible to draw on the facility for twice the amount it contributed.

The mechanics of the facility are as follows: drawings can be denominated in dollars, euros, or yen, and charges are based on the relevant London interbank offered rate (LIBOR). When a drawing is made, the lending countries credit the borrower for a corresponding amount in their central banks' books, denominated in the relevant currency. At the same time, the borrower credits the lenders an offsetting amount in its own central bank's books in the form of a noninterest-bearing account in the borrower's currency, but with the value of the entry maintained in terms of the currency in which the drawing is denominated. The AAB has never been used.

ASEAN Bilateral Repurchase Agreement (Repo)

Repurchase agreements have been negotiated between Indonesia and the four other original members of ASEAN. These involve a sale of US Treasury bills from the borrowing country to the lending country, with an agreement to reverse the transaction at a specified future date and at a predetermined price. The specific repurchase date, price, and procedures for the initiation and conclusion of the transactions are negotiated bilaterally by the two parties to the transaction. While the amounts involved can be large, the transactions are typically reversed in a short time (less than a month), and since Treasury bills are highly liquid, the facility does little to add to a country's stock of usable reserves.

The Chiang Mai Initiative

The Chiang Mai initiative (CMI) involves two components: an expanded ASA, and a series of bilateral swap arrangements (BSAs) between People's Republic of China, Japan, and Republic of Korea on the one hand, and the 10 members of ASEAN, on the other.

The ASA was expanded on 17 November 2000 to encompass all 10 ASEAN members and its total size was augmented. The 10 ASEAN countries were classified into two groups, corresponding to those under the AAB. Under the expanded arrangement, the six Group 1 countries would contribute $150 million each, while the four Group 2 countries would contribute as follows: Cambodia $15 million, Lao PDR $5 million, Myanmar $20 million, and Viet Nam $60 million, bringing the total size of the facility to $1 billion. The facility is available in dollars, euros, and yen, and the cost would be the corresponding LIBOR rate plus 25 basis points (bp). The maximum total period for each transaction is 6 months, and a cooling-off period of 6 months is imposed before a new drawing can be requested. Opt-out clauses are offered to participating countries if they are under International Monetary Fund (IMF) programs or have reserves equivalent to less than 3 months of imports.

Regarding the BSAs, each agreement would specify swaps in one of four forms: currency swap between the dollar and a local currency; currency swap between two local currencies (that of the borrowing country and of the lending Northeast Asian country—i.e., the yen, renminbi, or won); a repurchase agreement for US Treasury securities; and a repurchase agreement for a security denominated in the local currency of the Northeast Asian country. The period of the swap would be 90 days and it could be renewed up to seven times. The interest rate would be LIBOR plus 150 bp for the initial drawing and first renewal, with subsequent renewals paying an interest rate that increases by 50 bp for every two renewals, up to a maximum of 300 bp over LIBOR. Some 90% of the swap arrangements would be tied to existing IMF-supported programs, but the remaining 10% would not. The latter would be limited to only one renewal. Repurchase agreements would not be tied to IMF lending.

To date, 12 bilateral swaps have been successfully concluded with a combined total size of $31.5 billion, while two others are under negotiation (Table A1.1).

Table A1.1 **ASEAN+3 Bilateral Swap Arrangements (BSAs)**

BSA[a]	Currencies	Status	Amount
Japan-Korea	$/Won	Concluded / 4 Jul 2001	$2 billion
Japan-Thailand	$/Baht	Concluded / 30 Jul 2001	$3 billion
Japan-Philippines	$/Peso	Concluded / 27 Aug 2001	$3 billion
Japan-Malaysia	$/Ringgit	Concluded / 5 Oct 2001	$1 billion
PRC-Thailand	$/Baht	Concluded / 6 Dec 2001	$2 billion
Japan-PRC[b]	Yen/Renminbi	Concluded / 28 Mar2002	$3 billion
PRC-Korea[b]	Renminbi/Won	Concluded / 24 Jun 2002	$2 billion
Korea-Thailand[c]	$-Won/Baht	Concluded / 25 Jun 2002	$1 billion
Korea-Malaysia[c]	$-Won/Ringgit	Concluded / 26 Jul 2002	$1 billion
Korea-Philippines[c]	$/Peso	Concluded / 9 Aug 2002	$1 billion
PRC-Malaysia	$/Ringgit	Concluded / 9 Oct 2002	$1.5 billion
Japan-Indonesia	$/Rupiah	Concluded / 17 Feb 2003	$3 billion
PRC-Philippines		Under negotiation	
Japan-Singapore		Under negotiation	

PRC = People's Republic of China, Korea = Republic of Korea.

[a] In addition to the bilateral swaps is $7.5 billion that Japan is providing to Korea and Malaysia under the New Miyazawa Initiative.

[b] Two-way yen/renminbi swap arrangement.

[c] A two-way swap transaction of US dollar against the local currency.

References

Baig, Tamur. 2000. Characterizing Post-Crisis Exchange Rate Regimes in East Asian Economies. International Monetary Fund. September. (mimeo.)

Eichengreen, Barry. 2001. Hanging Together? On Monetary and Financial Cooperation in Asia, October. (mimeo.)

Frankel, Jeffrey, and Andrew Rose. 2002. An Estimate of the Effect of Common Currencies on Trade and Income. *Quarterly Journal of Economics* 117 (May): 437–466.

Hernandez, L. and Peter Montiel. 2002. Post-Crisis Exchange Rate Policy in Five Asian Countries. IMF Working Paper no. 01/170, International Monetary Fund.

McKinnon, Ronald I. 1999. The East Asian Dollar Standard: Life After Death? World Bank, February. (mimeo.)

________. 2000. After the Crisis, the East Asian Dollar Standard Resurrected: An Interpretation of High-Frequency Exchange Rate Pegging. Stanford University. (mimeo.)

Tenreyro, S. 2002. Economic Effects of Currency Unions. Harvard University, March. (unpublished)

Williamson, John. 2001. The Case for a Basket, Band and Crawl (BBC) Regime for East Asia. In *Future Directions for Monetary Policies in East Asia,* edited by David Gruen and John Simon. Sydney: Reserve Bank of Australia.

2 Information exchange, surveillance systems, and regional institutions in East Asia

Eric Girardin

Regional monetary and financial cooperation in East Asia can be undertaken in several ways. Aside from simple information sharing among participating countries, more structured forms of cooperation can include macroeconomic surveillance, reserve pooling, exchange rate targeting, and domestic financial sector restructuring and reform. Each of these forms of regional cooperation has an associated set of requirements, from mechanisms for information exchange and surveillance to supporting institutions.

This paper will assess existing initiatives with respect to these requirements at both the regional and global levels. It will suggest ways to address any gaps, by drawing in particular on the experience of the European Union (EU). The objective is to suggest institutional content for information exchange and surveillance in East Asia in the near future, as well as to consider how more structured forms of cooperation can be developed in the coming decades. In the process, certain constraints should be respected during this evolving process within the region.

This paper will argue that new types of regional institutional mechanisms should be developed to handle information exchange and surveillance, emphasizing flexibility and reactivity to the rapidly changing nature of the regional and international financial environment. They should promote transparency, allow policymakers to internalize the spillover effects of developments in their countries, promote the ownership of individual country reforms, enhance the quality of policy analysis and support, and give feedback on the extent of vulnerabilities of financial systems (Manzano 2001). The process of surveillance should involve (i) closely observing indicators of economic performance and policies, as well as early warning systems for potential financial risks; (ii) setting policy targets and designing incentive mechanisms for carrying out policies aimed at reaching such targets; and (iii) monitoring, which implies comparing the targets with actual performance (Ito 2002a; UN ESCAP 2001; Wang and Woo, volume 2). Accordingly, the analysis of surveillance should consider its effectiveness in identifying weaknesses and vulnerabilities; the substance of surveillance recommendations; and depending on their degree of implementation, the impact of such recommendations. Last, such analysis should also evaluate the conduct and methods of surveillance, i.e., the procedures through which surveillance is carried out.

The first section of this paper will examine the motivation for information exchange and surveillance at the regional level. It will consider alternative models for carrying out these activities in the separate areas of macroeconomic policy and financial sector restructuring. The second section will examine the lessons of European experience in these areas and consider the limitations of existing multilateral arrangements. The third section will assess East Asian initiatives as well as recent proposals for regional institution building for further information exchange and surveillance. The last section will put forward an action plan for the region.

Regional information exchange and surveillance: motivation and methods

Two broad issues should be addressed when examining the case for regional information exchange and surveillance: first, to what extent does the failure of market discipline justify international surveillance? Second, why should surveillance be conducted at the regional level rather than at the global level? This section will take up these questions, and will also consider the merits and demerits of alternative methods of regional information exchange and macroeconomic and financial surveillance.

Motives for and gains from international cooperation

Existing theory pinpoints three possible motives for international cooperation in information exchange and surveillance: macroeconomic interdependencies, financial crisis contagion, and common structural financial problems.

The presence of macroeconomic interdependencies and spillovers has traditionally been acknowledged as justifying surveillance and other forms of cooperation, such as liquidity provision and exchange rate coordination. On the other hand, contagion in financial crises is often considered as suggesting a need for financial cooperation. The usual focus of the rationale for cooperation is thus typically limited to interdependencies and contagion. However, purely informational spillovers among peers can just as well be a rationale. In particular, when countries' characteristics are correlated, there may be something to learn from the observation of similar economies via information sharing (Girardin, volume 2).

Each motive listed above yields specific gains from coordination that provide clear objectives for cooperation. These gains refer, respectively, to international macroeconomic stability, financial stability among the participating countries, and the reduction of systemic risk in domestic financial sectors.

Regional versus multilateral cooperation

The main advantage of regional peer monitoring over multilateral surveillance concerns the presumptions that neighboring and similar countries are better able to monitor each other than countries outside the region, and that they are in a better position to exert mutual informal pressures to comply with external mandates. Enforcement of such an implicit social contract can rely on mechanisms—such as the implied threat to discontinue interactions or the use of social sanctions—that may be more effective if issued by neighboring countries.

Moreover, such enforcement has the character of a public good. That is, in the absence of a delegated monitor, each country has an incentive to wait for another country to take the initiative of enforcement. This tendency to "free ride" is likely to be more pronounced in larger groups. Small regional groupings may thus have an enforcement advantage in this respect as well. Moreover, a regional monitor more directly responsive to the perspectives of participating countries (and thus with a better sense of ownership on the part of participating countries) may be more credible—and, thus, more effective—than one appointed at the global level.

Last, the development of shared common experience and group identity may foster a greater degree of trust among countries in a region, compared with that existing at the global level. This enhanced level of trust may generate specific benefits for monitoring. For example, it may help promote outcomes-based conditionality. This has the advantage that it limits interference in domestic affairs by leaving national authorities the choice of means to achieve agreed results. Such trust may be, in some fields, an alternative to costly policy-based monitoring in the early stages of regional macroeconomic cooperation.

Methods of regional cooperation

An adequate apparatus to detect the buildup of external macroeconomic vulnerabilities should be supplemented by efforts to make financial systems more robust and less vulnerable to shocks. But the scope and content of information exchange and surveillance may differ for macroeconomic and financial cooperation. As discussed above, the issue of enforcement mechanisms—such as the role of peer pressure or delegated monitoring versus trust—features prominently in coordination on macroeconomic matters (i.e., regional macroeconomic policy coordination, regional liquidity provision, and regional exchange rate arrangements). With financial cooperation, on the other hand, harmonization of standards becomes the central issue.

Harmonization of prudential standards, norms, and regulations at the regional level (based on adapted international standards) is often seen as the only avenue for regional cooperation for strengthening domestic financial systems. But financial cooperation need not imply the harmonization of standards. An alternative approach uses emulation for the spread of best practice and relies on self-control (Girardin, volume 2). Such "open" coordination is conceived as a process designed to help countries progressively develop their own financial policies. It is based on the recognition that many of the aims within the region are not (yet or at all) attainable through harmonization of regulations, but that they may still be of primary importance for countries to achieve better performance. Indeed, the underlying systems operated in various countries in a region may be so diverse that harmonization would require an effort quite disproportionate to the objectives and results to be achieved. The "open" method of coordination enables the different circumstances of each country to be taken into account and the timing of the policy mix to be adjusted by the national authorities to the needs of the various countries. Under this approach, countries work together voluntarily to align domestic rules, regulations, and standards with some indicative benchmark, which is agreed upon at the regional level. This is based on regional peer groups as fora for information exchange through mutual learning, and self-control or emulation.

The strategy of open coordination entails several steps. These include defining common objectives whenever countries decide that a certain field is a matter of common concern; fixing guidelines at the regional level, combined with timetables for achieving the stipulated goals; establishing qualitative and quantitative benchmarks against best practice (but tailored to regional or sectoral needs); and translating regional guidelines into national policies by setting targets and adopting measures tailored to national needs.

It is worth noting that, in contrast with financial sector reform, this method of open coordination is not well suited to the macroeconomic arena, where real interdependencies, as opposed to simple information spillovers, are at work. It is the appropriate method, for example, neither for regional crisis prevention and management nor for exchange rate coordination. Indeed, in those cases, it is certainly not adequate to let countries shop around and take decisions unilaterally without being subject to external pressure.

Lessons from the European experience and limitations of global initiatives

In this section, we will draw lessons from the EU experience in cooperation on macroeconomic and financial sector issues.[1] We will then consider the limitations of existing global financial arrangements.

Lessons from the experience of the European Union

During the regional integration process, European countries undertook both macroeconomic and financial coordination, with cooperation on the former taking precedence. The "Snake" arrangement (a reduction in fluctuation margins for some intra-EU member currencies) of the 1970s was followed by more structured exchange rate coordination in the exchange rate mechanism (ERM) period. Cooperation in this area involved exchange rate targeting and limited scope for surveillance. Aspects of the sanctions, peer pressure, and conditionality model of macroeconomic coordination were at work in some features of the ERM in a second macroeconomic area, that of liquidity provision. These became even more explicit later on, with the adoption of the Maastricht convergence criteria, followed by the Stability and Growth Pact. On the other hand, the self-control-in-regional-peer-groups model has been used by regulators and supervisors in the financial field.

[1] It may be tempting to look, in addition, into the experience of some other regional arrangements, such as the French franc zone in West and Central Africa. However, this would not be relevant to the East Asian situation, given that these arrangements involve asymmetric relationships, in which France adopts a role that creates a sort of fiscal federalism, enabling it to play a supervisory role in the "Comité monétaire," overseeing member countries' macroeconomic policies. See Kawai and Takagi (2000).

MACROECONOMIC COORDINATION

In its chapter on economic policy coordination, the Rome Treaty (1957, paras. 103–107) established the *Monetary Committee*, which comprised one representative from the central bank and one from the finance ministry of each member country, plus two representatives of the European Commission. The Monetary Committee proved a useful forum for information exchange and for preparation for the meetings of the Council of Ministers of Economics and Finance (ECOFIN). There was little effective macroeconomic cooperation during the 1960s, but since intra-European Economic Community (EEC) trade was still low (6% of gross domestic product [GDP] in 1960, doubling by 1975), this was not perceived as a particular problem.

A second forum for information exchange on monetary matters consisted of the *Committee of Governors* of central banks of member countries of the European Community, established in 1964. The committee held monthly meetings in the Bank for International Settlements (BIS) in Basle, in conjunction with the meetings of the governors of the central banks of the G-10 countries. It played a major role in the long process of monetary integration, enabling governors to exchange information and experiences and resolve technical issues that arose in their interaction.

Turbulence in the late 1960s and early 1970s led to exchange rate fluctuations, which were increasingly perceived as a threat to the European integration process (Boiscuvier and Steinherr, volume 2). As a result, the so-called Snake arrangement was adopted in April 1972. The adoption of the Snake arrangement was followed a year later by the creation of the European Monetary Cooperation Fund (FECOM), which was in charge of monitoring the Snake arrangement and assuring the multilateral nature of net interventions of participating central banks. One lesson of the EU experience, however, is that exchange rate targeting did not by itself imply substantial progress in information exchange and surveillance. Nonetheless, regular (up to monthly) meetings of EU central bankers, and ECOFIN, alone or jointly, over several decades, did ensure a growing familiarity and habit of working together (Gros and Thygesen 1998).

Alongside the somewhat hectic process of exchange rate coordination, one of the few by-products of the unsuccessful Werner Plan was, after March 1971, an effort to coordinate monetary and other macroeconomic policies more closely. For monetary policy, this involved the preparation of *general guidelines* by the Committee of Governors, to be followed by each member state, charting trends in bank liquidity and providing the terms for supply of credit and interest rates. This led to the establishment by the Governors' Committee of a Committee of Alternates and of Experts Groups to monitor trends in national money supplies and their main determinants, and a Working Group on Harmonization of Monetary Policy Instruments. However, this led only to a series of surveys, conducted by individual central banks, on the nature and use of monetary policy instruments, rather than to any formal mechanism for the coordination of monetary policies. The main outcome was instead a gradual but impressive increase in the exchange of information about domestic aspects of monetary policy.

In the 1980s, periods of exchange rate stability in the ERM were made possible by the use of capital controls, which provided the authorities with some degree of monetary policy independence, explaining the absence of a need for deeper information exchange and surveillance. Mutual surveillance was restricted to peer pressure during negotiations on realignments (which typically featured a return to purchasing power parity [PPP]) when their necessity appeared urgent (Boiscuvier and Steinherr, volume 2). External financial liberalization would have changed this situation, but that did not come until the end of the decade. Domestic financial liberalization was achieved only shortly before external liberalization.

The 1990s were characterized by the convergence process under the 1991 Maastricht Treaty. This experience in ensuring monetary stability involved the adoption of regional rules on domestic institution building, such as granting independence to central banks, together with the no-government-financing rule; and regional targets on intermediate and final objectives of monetary policy—convergence in levels of short-term interest rates and inflation rates.

Trust building through costly signaling was an important component of the monetary integration process in Europe throughout the 1980s and 1990s. Germany saw Italy, Spain, and, to a lesser extent, France, as high-inflation countries. It had little trust in the ability of these so-called "Club Med" countries to live without inflation. Agreeing to implement disinflation was thus a way for French, Italian, and Spanish authorities to send a costly signal to German authorities intended to reassure them and dispel their disbelief about the "Club Med" countries' commitment to price stability (on trust building through reassurance in international relations, see Kydd [2000]). This was first the case with the step-by-step hardening of the ERM, first after 1983 and then after 1987. Such a hardening was only made possible by painful domestic choices, entailing substantial costs, for benefits that would be slow to materialize. The "competitive disinflation" policy—associated in France with Jean-Clause Trichet—is an illustration, but it was only a by-product of the dramatic choice by President François Mitterand in March 1983, under the advice of Jacques Delors (then France's Finance Minister), not to leave the ERM. These costs were magnified when Germany's partners had to bear the negative spillover effects of German reunification, in the form of higher interest rates at a time of high unemployment, leading to further disinflation. In a similar way, Germany's partners enacted tough restrictive fiscal measures after the mid-1990s, which led to a successful fulfillment of the European Monetary Union (EMU) budget deficit criteria.

The different steps toward monetary integration in the EU shared certain common features (Boiscuvier and Steinherr, volume 2). One was a gradual path with adjustment costs, which, following the "economist" view, made it possible to better evaluate risks and learn from preceding mistakes.[2] Another was the genuine difficulty of reconciling the two main objectives of EU economic and monetary integration: catching up and price stability. Countries engaged in catching up must go through higher inflation; but ensuring price stability hampers domestic activity and prevents growth and catching up.

[2] It is arguable that relying on shock therapy, viewed in the "monetarist" approach as sending valuable signals to agents, may have permitted a faster move to monetary union.

In the EU, monetary and exchange rate stability came at the end of a long road that involved both deep trade integration, particularly with the free movements in the Single Market program as a crowning step, and considerable institution building (Chui et al 2002). A lengthy convergence process was the precondition for lasting monetary stability. The final emphasis, in the 1990s, on outcome-oriented convergence as opposed to policy-action convergence is a useful example of freedom of implementation of commonly agreed goals.

THE GROWTH AND STABILITY PACT

Successful regional surveillance was already at work in Europe in the 18 countries of the European Payments Union (EPU) in the 1950s (Kawai and Takagi 2000). To get financing to support the resolution of balance-of-payments disequilibria, countries had to meet specific conditions and to accept the monitoring of their domestic policy adjustments by the Managing Board of EPU. This was composed of financial experts reporting to the Council of the Organization for European Economic Cooperation (OEEC) (Gros and Thygesen 1998). However, such experience, which aimed at economizing international reserves at a time of dollar shortage and no capital account convertibility, is of little relevance for the current world with high international capital mobility.

Since the early 1990s, the main worry with regard to financial stability in the continental EU area (as reflected in the Delors Report) has focused on fiscal deficits and public debt. The central concern has been the spillover effects of public debt vulnerabilities. Default by a member country government was seen as the main regional systemic risk (Buiter et al 1993). This would involve negative externalities because the financial position of banks in the whole area holding government bonds would be at risk. There was also a risk that the central banks (and later the European Central Bank [ECB]) would have to play the role of a lender of last resort to rescue the EU banking system. It was felt that financial markets would not provide the right incentives to avoid this outcome. A market failure was seen to be at work inasmuch as a default risk premium was not charged to sovereign debtors whose public debt-to-GDP ratios reached much in excess of 100%.

Accordingly, regional targets for intermediate fiscal objectives were imposed in the form of ceilings on actual budget deficits and gross public debt (Boiscuvier and Steinherr, volume 2). In terms of regional financial surveillance,[3] in the 1990s, the EU thus put an exclusive emphasis on rules for fiscal discipline.

Independently of the process toward the EMU, many EU countries would have had to reduce their budget deficits and public debt, which had reached unsustainable levels in some cases. The reason why a (results-based) convergence process such as the Stability Pact, involving fiscal ceilings, could gain a consensus is that the regional goal of financial stability coincided with the domestic interest of member countries.[4]

To conclude this section, it is important to note that a key basis of macroeconomic surveillance in the European case has been the long elaboration of consistent statistics (Tetsuji 2002). There were strong roots, with the Statistical Office of the European Communities (*Eurostat*) in operation since 1953 and the publication of the European System of Integrated Economic Accounts (ESA) in 1970. The Single Market program had led in the late 1980s to the creation of the Statistical Programme Committee (SPC) in charge of joint actions and of the medium-term statistical programs. The Committee on Monetary, Financial and Balance of Payments Statistics assisted the European Commission in the first stage of EMU. The new European System of Accounts (ESA 95) was intended to meet the requirements for the implementation and the supervision of the EMU. The 1997 Treaty of Amsterdam even included articles on the production of

[3] Economic surveillance was to be conducted through regular convergence reports by the EU Commission, examined by ECOFIN. Broad economic policy guidelines were defined for member countries. The latter had to submit convergence programs, on a voluntary basis during the first stage and on a compulsory basis subsequently. Fines for noncompliance in case of breach of targets could be imposed. In the third stage, a crucial element is the political character of the decision by ECOFIN to impose such fines, which thus in no way have an automatic character.

[4] A similar rationale may be behind the recent initiatives in Latin America, both in the Andean Pact and MERCOSUR, also involving a macroeconomic convergence process. The convergence criteria in terms of inflation, fiscal deficits, and public debt are inspired by the Maastricht Treaty convergence criteria. They are mainly motivated by Latin America's record of chronic inflation and fiscal laxity. There is a clearly defined goal—a common market in subregions of Latin America in the medium term.

statistics. In the third stage of the EMU, the statistical requirements are magnified to ensure the surveillance of budgetary positions. The various stages of the deepening of regional surveillance thus required progress in building the statistical infrastructure.

COOPERATION BETWEEN DOMESTIC FINANCIAL AUTHORITIES

The strategy pursued by the EU on the regulation of financial services linked liberalization and regulation within the single market program. The decisive impetus was given by an EU 1985 White Paper that aimed at creating a *European financial area* by means of two series of crucial steps: the liberalization of capital movements as the necessary condition; and a novel package with respect to harmonization as the sufficient condition (Tsoukalis 1997).

Liberalization of capital flows was achieved through a first, timid directive in 1986, followed by a second, much more ambitious one, in 1988. The latter led to the complete elimination of capital controls in eight EU member states by July 1990.

The major regulatory breakthrough was the abandonment of any attempt to fully harmonize all rules and suppress home control. In its place, three major principles were agreed upon: *minimum harmonization*, strictly limited to essential rules; *mutual recognition* of national rules and regulations; and *home country* prudential control and *supervision* by the authorities of the country of origin of the bank. The crucial step was thus the acceptance of the principle of mutual recognition that reduced the role of harmonization to one of fulfilling basic requirements.

Three banking directives were adopted from April to December 1989 that then served as a model for other financial services, and came into effect at the beginning of 1993. They provided for the principles and definitions regarding banks' capital; established solvency ratios, with a weighted risk assessment of bank assets and off-balance sheet items, plus a harmonized minimum solvency ratio of 8% for credit institutions; and created a single banking license at the EU level. In the latter case, this implies that any bank that has been authorized by a competent authority of any EU member state can provide commercial as well as investment banking services across borders, and can also open branches in other EU member states. The regulations contained in the directives also cover the conditions for the opening and continuation of banking business, as well as accounting and control mechanisms. What were simply recommendations of the Basle Committee on Banking Supervision (BCBS) in 1988 were transformed into mandatory rules for EU-registered banks with some adaptations to EU needs, such as the definition of capital.

Prudential control of all branches of banks is left to the authorities where the parent company is based (home country), but the authorities of the host country share responsibility for supervising the liquidity of branches in their own territory. Thus, such a regulatory framework for financial services does not lead to the transfer of power to the EU level, after minimum common standards have been agreed upon.

Some useful lessons can be drawn from the EU experience in financial services regulation. A means had to be found to replace the many restrictions previously in place in the various countries. This led, in the EU, to the strong reliance on capital asset ratios (CARs) as a prudential control rule that could be widely applied. Moreover, relying on minimal harmonization implies the adoption of transparent and generally accepted regional common standards. A major issue is the scope for the applicability of such minimum common standards (such as CARs) because of the inherently diverse banking structures and regulatory traditions of member countries. Thus, the investment banking directive of 1993 and the capital adequacy directive of 1996 generalized to nonbank investment firms the right to the European passport, previously restricted to European banks.

FORUMS ON FINANCIAL SECTOR ISSUES

The EU has set up a number of forums, in the form of meetings of regulatory and supervisory authorities, in the three areas of banking, insurance, and securities. Such forums discuss prudential regulations, their practical implementation, and supervisory issues concerning specific financial institutions (EC 2000). There is a clear split between groups that are attached to EU institutions and those that are not formally linked to the EU, with a division of labor between the two types. In banking, for instance, the former never discuss issues relating to individual banks, unless their situation causes problems of such a dimension that prudential issues are at stake and require a response at the EU level, while the latter specialize in considering specific cases.

Attached to EU institutions are the Contact Groups with the European Commission for the regulation of supervision. This involves the advisory committees set up by EU directives: the Banking Advisory Committee (BAC) set up in 1977, the Insurance Committee (1991), and the Securities Contact Committee (Listing Admission Directive, 1979). For example, in banking, the Committee includes high-level representatives of member states' finance ministries, central banks, and supervisory authorities. Its role is to assist the European Commission in preparing prudential legislation for the supervision of the EU banking sector and to discuss and provide advice on other issues concerning banking regulation and supervision in the EU. The BAC, meeting quarterly, is empowered to adopt formal opinions on any proposal for EU banking legislation.[5] Such opinions are communicated to the commissioner in charge of banking regulation. Last, the BAC can amend technical provisions in EU banking directives.

A Banking Supervision Committee (BSC) was set up in October 1998 at the European System of Central Banks. The BSC, which meets five times a year and includes high-level representatives of member states' central banks and supervisory authorities, has two functions. It assists in the smooth conduct of supervisory and financial stability policies, which are examined from a macro-prudential perspective. It also provides assistance in the preparation of ECB's advice on proposals for EU and national banking legislation. The second main function is to act as a forum for the exchange of views and information among EU banking supervisors and central banks, and to examine developments or incidents in the EU banking systems of systemic or major relevance.

[5] EU legislation covers authorization requirements for banks (including minimum solvency requirements, large exposure, and the constitution of own funds); the manner in which banks are supervised (consolidated supervision for groups of credit institutions); the way in which cooperation between the banking supervisory authorities of the EU is conducted, the flow of information between banking supervisors themselves, and with other financial and nonfinancial authorities; and cross-border banking business and deposit guarantee schemes. The BAC establishes ratios for the solvency, liquidity, and profitability of credit institutions.

The major feature of this arrangement is the full application of the *subsidiarity principle*. Indeed, the BSC has no specific supervisory power. Supervisory authority remains at the national level. In its preparation of a framework for action for financial services, the European Commission stressed that it "considers that structured cooperation between national supervisory bodies, rather than the creation of new EU level arrangements, can be sufficient to ensure financial stability" (EC 1999, p. 2). However, it emphasized the need for supervisory authorities to strengthen cooperation so as to ensure application of a uniform understanding of prudential rules.

Not linked to EC are groupings of supervisors of member countries. In banking, the Groupe de Contact (GdC) was created in 1972, meeting at least three times a year. The main activity of the GdC is the confidential exchange of information on individual banking cases relevant to banking supervision. It is not formally attached to any EU institution, but its existence is explicitly acknowledged in EU banking directives. The composition of the GdC involves midmanagement banking supervisors of all EU member states, who are involved in the day-to-day supervision of banks. In addition, this group reviews developments in member countries' supervisory systems and prepares as well as discusses comparative reports, from the perspective of banking supervisors, on supervisory and regulatory issues. Upon request, or at its own initiative, it may also examine and prepare reports to be considered by the BAC or the BSC. In particular, the GdC annually reports on the observation of profitability and solvency ratios by the EU banking sector, for discussion in the BAC. The corresponding institution in the insurance sector is the Conference of Insurance Supervisory Authorities of the Member States of the European Union (set up in 1957), and for the securities industry, the High Level Securities Supervisors Committee (set up in 1985).

Soon after the start of the EMU, concern arose on the need for prudential supervision of an integrated financial system (Boiscuvier and Steinherr, volume 2). Under the aegis of the Economic and Financial Committee, a working group chaired by Dutch Deputy Governor Henk Bouwer examined supervisory arrangements for cross-border banking, and published its findings in two reports.

The first, in April 2000, focuses on arrangements for the prevention of regional financial crises. It recommends enhancement of the practical functioning of the institutional arrangements, by strengthening international cooperation and promoting information exchange between the main financial entities (large cross-border and cross-sectoral financial groups, and various authorities). The second, in April 2001, deals with financial crisis management and considers that closer cooperation among authorities (supervisors, central banks, and ministries) is required.

EU COEXISTENCE WITH MULTILATERAL ARRANGEMENTS

One of the major issues surrounding surveillance is how regional arrangements can work efficiently in areas where multilateral arrangements are in place. The interface between the two remains an open issue in many discussions about the prospects of East Asian cooperation. Many observers see a contradiction between the two, resulting in potential crowding out. In an analogy with Gresham's law, alleged inferior regional arrangements would crowd out good multilateral ones.

In the EU case, the interface with multilateral arrangements occurred when carrying out both macroeconomic and financial cooperation. When targeting the exchange rate in the Snake arrangement, the switch of the international monetary system from fixed rates to floating led to the disappearance of the tunnel, in which the Snake had been moving. But the Snake survived in its own right, showing for the first time that regional exchange rate targeting could fly in a world of floating. The previous experience of the 1930s had been more negative in this respect. However, the turbulence of the 1970s, with recurrent supply shocks and disorderly macroeconomic policy responses to them, illustrates the difficulties faced by such pioneering arrangements in their early stages, i.e., before they gather pace. Indeed, there were certainly backward steps along the way (France leaving the Snake in 1976, etc.).

European cooperation in regional liquidity provision showed that such arrangements (with or without conditionality) could survive very well and complement multilateral liquidity provisioning and conditionality. The very short-term and short-term financing facilities in the Snake, as well as in the ERM, were not linked to any conditionality (Gros and Thygesen 1998, p. 49). This is to be contrasted with the provision of liquidity by the International Monetary Fund (IMF) that is subject to approval and conditionalities, even when a country draws only the first tranches of its quota. This was true only of medium-term financing under the European arrangement. Such medium-term financial assistance in Europe included some procedures similar to those of IMF: conditionality and reimbursements in tranches on the basis of decisions by qualified majority in the ECOFIN council (Boiscuvier and Steinherr, volume 2). This credit facility had only limited bearing on the operation of the European Monetary System (EMS) proper. It was used on several occasions, but only to help medium-term balance-of-payments adjustment (Gros and Thygesen 1998, p. 67). The procedures for granting long-term financial support were toughened by the Maastricht Treaty in its Article 103a, which stipulated unanimity in decisions. Overall, the European experience shows that regional peer monitoring (ECOFIN) and delegated monitoring (supervision by the European Commission) can coexist with multilateral supervision by IMF.[6]

EU cooperation in financial sector reform is yet another example of the possibility of "cohabitation" between regional and multilateral arrangements: EU meetings of domestic regulators and supervisors as opposed to BIS meetings of such authorities. The high-level representatives of the central banks and banking supervisory authorities of eight member states of the EU (plus the commission and the ECB) are members of the BCBS. The role of the BCBS is to issue nonbinding, but authoritative, recommendations on the prudential supervision of banks. Such recommendations are generally translated into EU banking legislation, but what matters most is that this takes into account the nature of the EU banking sector.

For both areas of cooperation there is thus evidence of the possibility of complementarity between regional and multilateral

[6] The experience of the Andean Reserve Fund since the late 1970s and of the wider Latin American Reserve Fund since the early 1990s also show the possibility of such coexistence between conditionalities linked to regional short-term financing and conditionalities associated with multilateral financing.

arrangements. The careful design of regional institutions must have played a role in this successful cohabitation. It may at some stage have made obsolete some multilateral procedures, such as the disappearance of the need by EU countries for IMF liquidity provision; but this is the product of success, not of failure.

Global initiatives

The impetus for active integration in East Asia has come partly from the fact that multilateral organizations were not very successful in dealing with the 1997–1998 financial crisis. It also partly resulted from the observation that multilateral cooperation, far from making substantial progress toward the elusive goal of reforming the international financial architecture, has instead focused on efforts to design very elaborate standards and codes of conduct, the implementation of which is left to the discretion of national authorities.

GLOBAL SURVEILLANCE FORUMS

Traditional forums for surveillance at the global level include annual Article IV reviews by IMF of all member countries (Ito 2002a). The assessment is focused on macroeconomic issues (for example, the stance of monetary and fiscal policies), conditions in financial markets, and the balance of payments. This is supplemented by more intense monitoring of economic policies and conditions in countries that receive IMF financing.

Surveillance is also conducted by other multilateral organizations, such as the Organisation for Economic Co-operation and Development (OECD). OECD not only conducts annual reviews of its members, but also undertakes thorough surveillance activities in the Working Party (WP3) of its Economic Policy Committee. This involves frank discussions and detailed coverage of macroeconomic developments in, among others, the East Asian region and emerging market countries. This is a useful model, but only 11 advanced countries are involved.

In addition, the Group of Seven (G-7) meeting of finance ministers (deputies) has been a major forum for the discussion of global and regional issues. This was enlarged in the 1990s—as a response to the proliferation of crises—to large emerging market countries that are acknowledged to have "systemic importance" for the stability of the global financial system. The resulting forum was designated the G-20. However, many East Asian countries are not involved in this forum.

RECENT REFORMS

After the recent spate of financial crises around the world, the issue of reforming multilateral financial institutions has come to the fore. On prevention, management, and resolution of international financial crises, in light of the recommendations of the *External Evaluation of IMF Surveillance* (Crow et al 1999), efforts have focused on improving, strengthening, and increasing the effectiveness of IMF procedures and instruments. These can be achieved through greater transparency of IMF operations, new financing facilities (the Supplementary Reserve Facility and Contingent Credit Line), and streamlining structural conditionalities (Kuroda and Kawai 2002).

A change of perspective in IMF conditionality has become evident (IMF 2001a). Initially, it was designed for countries facing a current account crisis that might lead to speculative attacks on a pegged exchange rate. Liquidity would be provided, on condition that macroeconomic policies would be tightened to bring the current account back to balance through a cut in absorption and a change in its composition. With the crises of the second half of the 1990s, which were capital account crises that destabilized exchange rates, a large set of structural conditions has tended to be attached to liquidity provision by IMF. Such conditions involve, in particular, restructuring and reforming the domestic financial system, especially the banking system. The unfortunate by-product of this has been to blur the distinction between the objectives of monetary and financial stability. Indeed, structural conditions require domestic authorities to use measures to restore financial stability so that they could have access to international liquidity, which will enable them to maintain monetary stability.

Since the middle of the 1980s, forums have played an active role in regulating the financial services industry at the global level to promote information exchange and develop standards. This has been most evident, because of the famous 1988 Basel prudential ratio produced by the BCBS, in the banking sector meeting on the premises of BIS. However, similar fora have been at work in the insurance sector with the International Association of Insurance Supervisors (IAIS), and in the securities industry, with the International Organization of Securities Commissions (IOSCO). Such organizations are not involved in surveillance, but specialize in regulation.

In the wake of recent financial crises, multilateral institutions have been preoccupied with defining a wealth of standards and codes of conduct in the areas of data dissemination, fiscal transparency, monetary and financial policy transparency, banking supervision, insurance and securities market regulation, and payments systems. Although this is valuable work, it may be too detailed and not suited to the needs of at least some East Asian countries. Moreover, even when they formally adopt them, such countries may lack the incentives (or simply the accounting and supervisory infrastructure) for actual implementation. There are even difficulties associated with the methodology with which the data are collected and analyzed. Such standards are the product of a top-down approach and do not take into account the fact that countries have different levels of financial development, different financial systems and structure, and different economic systems. Not enough consideration has been given to the issue of sequencing in the adoption of standards (no benchmark sequence[s]) in line with financial deepening and liberalization, or to adaptation to the regional characteristics of financial systems. It has thus tended to be a one-size-fits-all approach.

Jointly with the World Bank, IMF has developed financial sector assessment programs (FSAPs) aimed at identifying the strengths and vulnerabilities of a country's financial system (IMF 2000), as well as reports on the observance of standards and codes where participation is voluntary (IMF 2001b). There is some intention to link the FSAPs to IMF surveillance.

Other initiatives have led multilateral agencies to cooperate with global forums (G-7) and regulatory agencies within the Financial Stability Forum (FSF) to pool and share information on vulnerabilities in the international financial system, as well as to perform some degree of monitoring of the implementation of internationally agreed regulatory and supervisory standards and codes of conduct (UN ESCAP 2001, p. 199). Such initiatives have proven valuable in identifying regulatory gaps and vulnerable areas in the international financial system. However, the FSF raises little sense of concern or ownership in the region since it does not involve a large number of East Asian countries. The recent FSF meeting in East Asia, with the involvement of some additional countries of the region, may go some way toward correcting these weaknesses.

Overall, there is a gap between the improvements made at the multilateral level and the huge efforts required by authorities at the national level to adopt standards and codes, giving rise to some malaise in emerging countries (Lamberte 2001). There is thus ample room for regional initiatives in East Asia, especially when models of best practice defined at the multilateral level may serve as useful starting points to define regional benchmarks.

Gaps in East Asian initiatives and proposals

Since the 1997 crisis, there have been several initiatives in East Asia to start and strengthen regional economic cooperation. Also, various proposals have been put forward to provide institutional support for such initiatives. The present section will identify the gaps in these regional initiatives and assess such proposals.

A "natural" reluctance to regional legalization in Asia?

Many observers see a reluctance in East Asia to legalize regional links. This should be examined in the light of both theory and historical experience. On the theoretical side, there are four competing explanations of the legalization process of international institutions. Two of these help explain the current low level of institutionalization in East Asia, while the others suggest factors that would tend to support increased legalization in the region. On the empirical side, the actual experience of institution building in the region through the Association of Southeast Asian Nations (ASEAN) and Asia-Pacific Economic Cooperation (APEC)[7] shows that such a process has been multifaceted and characterized by substantial diversity in terms of legalization. Favorable factors for legalization, which have been at work in the past in East Asia, may well be operative again in the future.

THE PROS AND CONS OF REGIONAL LEGALIZATION

Regional institutions may tend to reflect domestic legal culture and institutions. Resistance to legalization may thus be culturally grounded in so-called "Asian values": "less adversarial and litigious, less intent on demonstrating right and wrong, more concerned with avoiding conflict" (Kahler 2000, p. 560). The Asian way would instead emphasize group harmony, consensus, or informality and would avoid legalism. International preferences would express "deep-seated cultural norms" (Kahler 2000, p. 560) that are reflected in domestic legal practices. However, it is difficult to find strong foundations to base an interpretation of international institutional design on a dominant legal culture. Indeed, "Most Asian societies, particularly in Southeast Asia, display legal pluralism rather than monolithic legal cultures and homogenous legal institutions" (Kahler 2000, p. 560).

An alternative explanation for the low degree of legalization in East Asia rests with domestic politics (Kahler 2000). Under this interpretation, developing countries in East Asia are perceived as sharing a common assessment of the high sovereignty costs of legalization. Other domestic political variables, such as political heterogeneity, may bias attitudes against institutional reform and development, especially when changing institutions requires reaching a consensus among participating countries. Consensus decision making protects national prerogatives, in a similar way to the absence of external binding constraints.

Among the arguments that support further legalization of regional economic institutions in East Asia, on the other hand,

[7] ASEAN is composed of 10 countries: Brunei Darussalam, Indonesia, Malaysia, Philippines, Singapore, Thailand, and Viet Nam, as well as Cambodia, Lao People's Democratic Republic, and Myanmar. The first seven are also members of APEC, which includes, in addition, American and Oceanian countries.

the first is demand-driven or functionalist. It emphasizes increasing economic integration and the rising intensity of regional economic relations. "As levels of integration grow, the binding character of liberalizing agreements becomes more important, and, as levels of obligation and precision increase, delegation of rule interpretation and adjudication of disputes is often observed" (Kahler 2000, p. 550). Given the rise in economic integration over the last decade and the prospective strengthening of this process, this view suggests that we should see a rise in demand for legalization in East Asia.

The other argument in favor of further legalization rests on the view that the choice of legalization is both instrumental and strategic (Kahler 2000). It is instrumental inasmuch as legalizing international economic institutions is a means to accomplishing other national ends. Since East Asian governments share common goals (economic integration) and common concerns, such as financial instability, the choice of legalization results from a calculus that legalized institutions serve those goals, even when (sovereignty) costs are taken into account. It is strategic because such a choice depends mostly on the competing strategies of other actors and their capabilities in the prospective institutional setting.

It is likely that the reluctance in East Asia to legalize regional links reflects both domestic legal culture and institutions (Asian values), as well as the awareness of the high sovereignty costs of legalization. However, there is increasing regional support for further regional legalization without supranationality, which may serve the common goal, increasingly shared in the region, of further integration and avoidance of financial crises. This is based on the realization that the net benefit of such cooperation may be positive even when sovereignty costs are properly taken into account.

ASEAN VERSUS APEC APPROACH TO LEGALIZATION

The East Asian experience with economic institution building has been characterized by a long evolutionary process of increasing legalization in the case of ASEAN and a much looser type of association in the case of APEC (Kahler 2000). These two different experiences provide support for the last two explanations of legalization.

Economic collaboration among ASEAN countries was initially rather limited. It began to develop when liberalization boosted the degree of economic interdependence among participating economies. The institutional form was intergovernmental and informal, based on a multilateral declaration rather than a treaty. ASEAN institutions have developed slowly. The basic principles were consultations, with decisions emerging from the bottom up, and characterized by consensus and unanimity. A small step from intergovernmental to transgovernmental collaboration was reached at the Manila summit in 1987 with the creation of a Senior Economic Officials Meeting to handle economic cooperation. The ASEAN Free Trade Area (AFTA) did not involve creating formal regional institutions or negotiating precise and binding obligations. This reflected the different levels of income and industrialization of member countries, as well as inward-looking economic policies.

AFTA illustrated the possibility of at least some slow progress in legalization in two ways. It involved expanded delegation, with the ASEAN secretariat being given increased responsibilities for initiating, advising, coordinating, and implementing ASEAN activities. It also allowed the Senior Economic Officials to recommend decisions to the economic ministers on the basis of "flexible consensus," which represented a departure from the unanimity principle that had been the rule in ASEAN. However, lack of precision, giving rise to ambiguities and contested interpretations, remained a major problem, as illustrated by the lack of concrete and specific provisions in the AFTA founding document, which contained no more than 15 pages, in contrast with the 1,000 pages of the North American Free Trade Agreement (NAFTA).

The Kushing Consensus laid the ground rules for ASEAN participation in APEC. Although it stipulated that no mandatory directives should be adopted within APEC, it provided that legalization could go forward through one of two routes: (i) agreements on nonbinding principles, which could develop into a more binding code; and (ii) allowing opt-out clauses, enabling some countries not to participate in more binding agreements.

Developing country members of APEC at the Bogor Summit supported the strengthening of the process through unilateral means. Adding peer pressure within APEC councils would lead to Concerted Unilateral Action (CUA) but would stop short of binding commitments or deadlines, extensive monitoring, or the application of sanctions (Kahler 2000). APEC's East Asian members (and some Eminent Persons Group reports) proposed an APEC dispute mediation service rather than a dispute settlement mechanism. This aimed at reflecting the absence of agreed rules against which to judge compliance and the low degree of comparability of domestic laws among the participating economies.

East Asian initiatives after 1997

A multiplicity of groupings has recently emerged in East Asia, characterized by variable geometry both in scope and membership, sometimes extending to countries outside the region. A core group of seven countries (henceforth, EA-7) from East Asia (People's Republic of China [PRC], Indonesia, Japan, Republic of Korea [Korea], Malaysia, Singapore, and Thailand) is found in all groupings. Current initiatives can be assessed on the basis of both the content of information exchange (priorities, targets, etc.) and the conduct and methods of surveillance, as well as the substance and implementation of recommendations in the peer review process (Wang and Woo, volume 2).

REGIONAL MACROECONOMIC SURVEILLANCE

Regional macroeconomic surveillance in East Asia is a new process that started 5 years ago after the onset of the financial crisis. The track record of the different surveillance mechanisms and forums is, of course, necessarily limited over such a short period. In order to assess the achievements to date as well as the challenges ahead, a natural starting point is a diagnosis of the gaps in the regional surveillance process prior to the crisis. Four of them have been identified (Manzano 2001): a lack of transparency due to the absence of information flows, weaknesses in the surveillance models used, obstacles to carrying out surveillance recommendations, and widespread financial sector vulnerabilities.

First, prior to the crisis, there was little opportunity at the regional level for disclosing adequate and timely information about existing conditions, policy decisions, and actions. This weakened market discipline and did not allow any type of peer review process other than on a very vague basis. Second, models used in the global surveillance mechanisms did not allow the tracking of vulnerabilities, let alone the provision of early warning. Moreover, global surveillance had an excessively narrow focus, in particular leaving out the financial system. Third, even if such tools had been available, serious obstacles would have prevented regional forums from exerting effective peer pressure on countries where vulnerabilities were identified. A tradition of noninterference in other countries' domestic affairs would have prevented the carrying out of surveillance recommendations by regional forums. Only by ensuring enough ownership of the surveillance process by participating countries could such obstacles have been overcome. Fourth, even if remedial policies had been taken, they might have had little impact because some vulnerabilities had already built up to such levels that only preemptive policy actions could have made a real difference.

After the 1997–1998 crisis, attempts at regional financial cooperation through surveillance in East Asia have built on APEC and ASEAN+3, involving the PRC, Japan, and Korea.

The *Manila Framework Group* (MFG) under APEC, created in November 1997, aims to provide some degree of regional surveillance as a complement to the global surveillance exercised by IMF. It is also designed to provide technical assistance to enable countries to strengthen their financial systems.

The MFG did not substantially contribute to filling the surveillance gaps seen in East Asia prior to the crisis. Transparency has not been a major concern, the objectives of surveillance have not been specified, no surveillance systems have been established, neither the basis nor the outcome of discussions are made public, and no genuine peer review process is at work. In effect, the MFG is simply a forum for discussing regional and global perspectives, rather than a framework for formulating recommendations for policy actions.

Other reasons for questioning the effectiveness of the MFG (Ito 2002a) include the fact that its meetings do not have a specific agenda, but depend on the agenda in global (G-20, FSF, IMF) or regional (APEC, ASEAN) discussions. There is no "common stake" to the MFG. Twice-yearly meetings are too infrequent, and the lack of a permanent secretariat is a major drawback.

The *ASEAN surveillance process* and *ASEAN+3* Economic Review and Policy Dialogue Process also pursue regional macroeconomic stability. The ASEAN surveillance process started in 1998 with the ASEAN Surveillance Coordinating Unit (ASCU) attached to the Secretariat in Jakarta. National surveillance units in six countries provide draft chapters for the surveillance report (Rana 2002). The Asian Development Bank (ADB) provides technical assistance as well as inputs to the surveillance report, which is prepared by ASCU. The confidential draft surveillance report is examined at ASEAN Finance Ministers and Central Bank Deputies' Meetings and then finalized. The final stage is the Finance Ministers' Meetings, conceived as the forum for information exchange and discussion, peer review on the basis of the *Economic Outlook* and the surveillance report, the design of policy options, the encouragement of corrective actions both at the domestic and at the collective level, and the monitoring of regional or global developments. The end product can be regional or national measures that would find expression in a joint ministerial statement (Rana 2002).

The ASEAN surveillance process has thus gone some way toward filling some surveillance gaps existing prior to the crisis. Transparency of information has started to improve, surveillance instruments have been established, and a peer review process has to some extent been initiated.

The most promising development involves the ASEAN+3 Economic Review and Policy Dialogue process. The ASEAN+3 group (which itself was created in November 1999) has held surveillance-process Finance Ministers' Meetings twice a year since May 2000. Such a process is analogous to ASEAN surveillance. The process involves monitoring capital flows; preparing surveillance report; developing parametric and nonparametric early warning systems for the five crisis-affected countries (Indonesia, Korea, Malaysia, Philippines, and Thailand); formulating leading indicators of business cycles (for Malaysia and the Philippines); and creating a core set of macroprudential indicators for ASEAN countries plus the PRC and Korea, covering six broad categories (current account, capital account, financial sector, fiscal account, real sector, and global economy).

The Regional Economic Monitoring Unit (REMU) at ADB maintains a web site—the Asia Recovery Information Center (ARIC)—with detailed macroprudential indicators, and produces the *Asia Economic Monitor*, which replaced the *Asia Recovery Report* in late 2001, and now features a section on financial restructuring. In the light of the surveillance and vulnerability reports, surveillance is exercised twice a year by peer review at the ASEAN+3 Finance Ministers' Meetings, and the Finance Ministers and Central Bank Deputies' Meetings. The ADB Institute in Tokyo (supplemented by the Asian Policy Forum) conducts in-depth studies, in particular on macroeconomic and financial issues in the region.

When assessing the ASEAN+3 Economic Review and Policy Dialogue process, encouraging signs, similar to those in the ASEAN process, are apparent. Surveillance gaps have begun to be filled by initiating a process of greater transparency and flow of information through the design of an extensive range of vulnerability and early warning indicators (with promising results); as well as with the consciousness of the need to develop mechanisms for carrying out surveillance recommendations.

However, given its short track record, this process is subject to several limitations (Wang and Woo, volume 2). First, concerning transparency, the required content of information exchange is not specified in detail. In the absence of any required minimum common set of data to be provided, countries are left with substantial discretion over the information they release. This makes it difficult to conduct a mutually beneficial exchange of views and experience. Second, the early warning system does not give sufficient attention to regional interdependencies and contagion, since it focuses on a country-by-country approach. Third, the leading indicators of business cycles could usefully be expanded to a larger set of countries, including in particular the PRC. Fourth, while discussions do take place on recent developments in member countries, they do so only on a voluntary basis. As yet the peer review process involves neither enough substance in surveillance recommendations nor a mechanism for monitoring the actual implementation of recommendations.

Under the *Chiang Mai Initiative* (CMI) of the ASEAN+3 Finance Ministers (May 2000), the surveillance process has been supplemented by regional financial support (Chaipravat, this volume). The latter has been arranged to back currency support policies, intending to fill gaps left by multilateral financing in terms of speed and amount of disbursements. However, no regional conditionality has been designed, since external delegated monitoring has been favored for the bulk (90%) of the regional financing, which has been made conditional on IMF programs. Moreover, when providing one tenth of the swap facility, the countries themselves have to assess the conditions in the states benefiting from the facility. One obvious limit of such arrangements is that assessment is likely to be made on a purely discretionary basis, without common principles agreed at the regional level.

The ASEAN+3 Study Group at its first meeting in Malaysia in late 2001 examined "the possible modalities to enhance the effectiveness of economic reviews and policy dialogues among ASEAN+3 countries." Strengthening a regional surveillance mechanism was agreed upon in two steps (Wang and Woo, volume 2). The first step involves informal and voluntary meetings around the annual meetings of IMF/World Bank. Participating countries will circulate a brief report on their recent economic developments, according to a format to be specified, with possible inclusion of IMF/World Bank/ADB assessments. The second step would involve the formal designation of some institutional support for the assessment (as a supplement to IMF surveillance), based on an enhanced ASEAN secretariat, an existing institution, or a working group. Wang and Woo (volume 2) argue that the second option seems the more desirable.

REGIONAL FINANCIAL SURVEILLANCE

Turning to the financial arena, *cooperation among domestic financial authorities* has taken place only on a tentative level.

Regional meetings of regulators and supervisors do occur, but with a low frequency and without a clear agenda and timetable. In addition, the Executive Meeting of East Asian and Pacific Central Banks (EMEAP), which includes 11 central bank governors from the Asian and Pacific region (i.e., EA-7 plus Australia; Hong Kong, China; New Zealand; and Philippines) has been taking place annually since 1996. It focuses on special themes such as monetary policy and asset prices, or international investment and financial stability. Their deputies have been meeting twice a year since 1991. It also features working groups on subjects such as payments and settlement systems, financial markets, and banking supervision. EMEAP was the framework for the signing of bilateral repurchase agreements in the mid-1990s. Other central bank fora include an ASEAN Central Bank Forum, SEANZA (Southeast Asia, New Zealand, Australia), which has been in existence since the mid-1950s, and SEACEN (Southeast Asian Central Banks) created in the mid-1960s.

Institutional proposals for East Asia

The proposals that have been put forward for further regional institution building in East Asia vary in scope, membership, and degree of legalization.

An *expanded EMEAP* would build on its close links with BIS and IMF (Rajan 1999). The scope of EMEAP would be widened by focusing on its original goals of enhancing regional financial and monetary cooperation as well as by offering support for currencies in the region facing speculative pressures. The use of a monetary facility involving the pooling of reserves would be based on conditionality in two ways, involving a mixture of the preselection model and policy actions-based conditionality (on these, see Girardin [volume 2]). Member economies would have to satisfy, in a continuous way, predetermined standards of macroeconomic and financial stability, and stand ready to undertake necessary policy adjustments, subject to peer monitoring. Existing arrangements would need to be supplemented by peer review and an effective regional surveillance process, with early warning signals tracking national, regional, and international macroeconomic developments. The ASEAN surveillance process would have to be expanded to include non-ASEAN members of EMEAP and be integrated in the latter. The main downside of such a proposal is that it involves only central bankers, it includes countries outside the ASEAN+3, particularly from central Asia and Oceania, and it does not build on trade-integrating institutions.

An *Asian BIS* is seen as bearing two responsibilities (for Rajan [1999], this could be the second step after the strengthening of EMEAP): to develop regionwide banking and financial standards and codes consistent with international best practices, and to monitor their implementation.

Apart from providing aid to regional currencies susceptible to speculative pressures (ADBI 2000), an *Asian Monetary Fund (AMF)* would have a surveillance role at the regional level. It would particularly be involved in crisis prevention, possibly leaving crisis management and resolution to IMF (Rajan 2000).

The *Asian Financial Institute* (AFI), championed by Eichengreen (2001), would combine the activities of an Asian BIS and an AMF. It would first coordinate initiatives for promoting financial stability and development in the East Asian region, through technical assistance, training, and provision of central banking services (reserve management, clearing, and settlement). It would be the venue for the negotiation on agreements on a distinct set of regional capital and liquidity requirements and regulatory processes, and on standards for information disclosure. The second series of tasks of the AFI would be, first, to coordinate monetary, fiscal, financial, and regulatory policies, so as to promote the development of financial markets in the region; and, second, to provide emergency assistance (credits and swaps) to countries experiencing financial difficulties of a regional systemic character. Under Eichengreen's blueprint, the geographical grouping for such an institute would be the ASEAN+3 members.

Unfortunately, such proposals seem too ambitious and, for at least one of the following reasons, are doomed to fail. First, they involve an unnecessary concentration of responsibilities and power in a single institution, and they generally do not acknowledge the need for an approach by stages (Ito 2002a). In short, they propose considerable institution building. Given the constraints under which cooperation in East Asia tends to operate—especially taking into account the reluctance to legalize at the regional level—a much more decentralized approach to cooperation seems preferable in the near future. Second, almost all these proposals see regional *harmonization* of standards, codes, and regulations as the only possible route, and miss the alternative approach of adopting more flexible forms of cooperation, possibly laying the basis for mutual recognition.

Action plan for information sharing and surveillance in East Asia

Given that the ASEAN+3 countries have shown willingness to cooperate, it would seem to be the right grouping to strengthen cooperation even if, along the road, some subregional groups emerge around some common concerns. Based on the analysis of the deficiencies of existing regional cooperative arrangements, this section will lay out a road map for improved regional information sharing and surveillance in East Asia in the macroeconomic and financial arenas. The action plans are divided into successive phases, each of which builds on the accomplishments of the previous phase.

A road map for enhanced regional macroeconomic surveillance

PHASE ONE

Within the CMI, East Asian countries should build a framework for an enhanced dialogue on policies to strengthen regional surveillance mechanisms (Wang and Woo, volume 2). As a first step, this involves introducing a system for sharing information so as to increase the transparency of domestic economic policies in a peer review process. Capacity building for this purpose would be provided, through technical assistance, by advanced countries in the region or existing regional multilateral institutions.

With respect to the scope and content of this enhanced process of information sharing, we can divide it into three parts.

First, a common template should be designed for the reports that are now voluntarily prepared by each member of ASEAN+3. Data on external accounts, monetary and financial accounts, fiscal positions, and real sector resilience may usefully be supplemented by data on several variables (poverty rates, industrial action, and political developments) as well as major institutional and legal changes. This would give deeper information on the resilience of member countries' economies. Economic reports should include ADB, IMF, and World Bank assessments as well as countries' responses to them and possibly private sector (international credit rating agencies and global investment companies) reports.

Second, macroprudential indicators and early warning systems that have been designed and developed at the regional level should be deepened by putting more emphasis on regional linkages. The work on leading indicators of the business cycle would benefit from taking into account regional co-movements in forecasting economic activity. Such initiatives should be accompanied by "real time" indicators, focused on high frequency (daily) movements of regional financial markets. This would imply the development of financial market stress indicators to measure the short-term buildup of tensions and vulnerabilities. One could consider three markets (stocks, interest rate, and currency), and four symptoms of tensions in financial systems: volatility in the price of financial assets, liquidity risk, reassessment of credit risk, and volatility transmission. Each member country would have to contribute its own cell based on a standard methodology for computing the stress index (similar to the signals approach in early warning systems). The resulting spreadsheet would be confidential but available to all member countries' authorities periodically, say every week during periods of turmoil. Using available high-frequency (even daily) data on portfolio flows to and from some G-3 countries (mainly the United States), some matching information on capital flows could also be usefully gathered on a regular basis.

Third, given the wide diversity of frameworks for monetary policies that exist, a regional exchange rate arrangement is probably not on the agenda for the near future. However, uncertainties about exchange rate policy may have destabilizing effects in the meantime. Thus, the enhanced effort to achieve transparency in the region should extend to the authorities in charge of exchange rate policy, in order to reduce such uncertainties. It is desirable for countries to inform each other about the objectives of their exchange rate policies, as well as the specifics of their interventions in the foreign exchange market. Some gradual progress toward similar modes of intervention may even be possible in the short run as a step toward a more cooperative exchange rate policy later on. The possibility of joint intervention should be examined and discussed among countries in the region.

A network of East Asian decision makers in the field of exchange rate intervention should enhance formal and informal policy dialogues and possibly gradually design and put in place mechanisms for exchange rate policy coordination. This would help set the stage for negotiations for later steps toward exchange rate coordination in the region.

To prepare decision makers for such developments, discussion and exchange of information in the short run should cover not only the objectives of monetary policy, but also the operational framework of such policy, including targets, instruments, and procedures. The fora should include a Committee of Governors of Central Banks of East Asia, meeting monthly; a Monetary Committee formed on the basis of meetings of the ASEAN+3 Finance and Central Banks Deputies, occurring twice per quarter; and an ASEAN+3 Economic and Finance Ministers' Meeting, which should be held every quarter. The Monetary Committee should establish surveys of monetary policy frameworks in the region.

An East Asian regional Macroeconomic and Financial Statistics Agency is required to back all of these initiatives. Such an agency should focus on both macroeconomic and financial sector data and gather consistent data for all East Asian countries and on regional indicators. It would involve high-level officials and experts discussing both the data needs for surveillance at the regional level as well as some common template for producing statistics.

In this first phase, information sharing would be the major product. No attempt would necessarily be made to reach consensus on solving problems. Increased transparency, however, should be conducive to a substantial improvement in mutual confidence.

PHASE TWO

Peer pressure through information exchange and discussion in a regional forum should gradually be replaced by delegated monitoring at the regional level when the secretariat has acquired sufficient capacity. Such an independent surveillance unit would lead the regional policy dialogue, acting as a warehouse and processor of information, and provider of early warning signals. On this basis, it would draft its own surveillance report identifying major issues to be discussed within the policy dialogue framework. The latter would make implied policy recommendations to member countries, which would be included in a specific chapter of the surveillance report. The implementation of such recommendations would thus not simply rely on peer pressure. By also being made public, this pressure would be reinforced by financial market monitoring—i.e., countries not carrying out the recommendations would be subject to market discipline. Besides, such countries would not be eligible for CMI benefits.

As improved information exchange and surveillance puts the region in a better position to design and monitor its own conditionality, the share of short-term financing within CMI that is not linked to IMF programs could rise over time. This conditionality should address macroeconomic as well as financial sector issues. In particular, for other participants in the CMI to grant a country financial support, the applicant would have to show that it already meets a number of criteria on financial sector reform.[8] Subsequently, to get a renewal of its facility, it would need to show that it has made substantial progress in bringing in standards, codes, and practices. Such progress could only be made at the margin, assuming that the process of implementing them had already

[8] There is indeed agreement in the CMI that all swaps would take into account "economic conditions" of the country requesting them.

started beforehand. Consequently, this phase of macroeconomic surveillance would have to wait until phase two of the agenda for regional financial cooperation recommended below is reached.[9]

Regional conditionalities should be much streamlined compared with those of IMF. It is true that IMF itself has been streamlining its own set of structural conditionalities, but even compared to this benchmark, East Asia needs a reduced set of more clearly defined "conditions." Such regional "conditions" should meet three requirements. First, they should be tailored to the characteristics of East Asian countries (e.g., bank-based financial systems), which would be made possible by the active participation of the relevant countries in the design of conditions, allowing a genuine sense of ownership. Second, they should be linked to a wider East Asian regional effort at designing its own standards, codes, and rules of good practice. Third, regional conditionality should be results-oriented and not based on policy actions. This would enable the use of off-site supervision instead of on-site missions.

As the CMI possibly develops toward some form of independent reserve pooling institution, the ASEAN+3 surveillance unit would have to expand in scale. Technical expertise and financial and human resources of the surveillance unit would have to be enhanced to enable it to conduct quality and in-depth analysis of regional economic problems.

PHASE THREE

In case a clear and explicit policy of exchange rate targeting is adopted in the region (or subregion), its implementation should wait until phase three of the regional agenda for financial cooperation described below, since conditions have to be met for regional exchange rate stability to be possible. Given the twin character of financial crises (embracing both banking and currencies), dealing with the prevention of banking crises should

[9] Obviously, it would not make much sense to ask for a set of standards, codes, and good practices in the financial sector to be met at the time when liquidity is provided through the CMI swap arrangements, if there had not been prior regional efforts at designing and installing them.

eventually limit the likelihood of speculative attacks. This would provide a firm basis on which to design outcome-oriented financial convergence criteria (possibly involving ceilings on bank credit growth and asset price inflation) with a clear timetable, ensuring financial system soundness.

Regional cooperation on financial sector issues

Independently of any regional macroeconomic cooperation, there is an acknowledged need for almost all countries in the region, from the largest to the smallest ones, to finalize the restructuring of their banking systems as well as to progress in developing their prudential and supervisory apparatus. They have started doing this independently and without coordination. There is thus ample room for building a consensus at the regional level for choosing the domestic financial field as a key area for cooperation.

Given that this is a new area of regional cooperation, there is a need to devise new methods to address it. The lack of a supranational dimension in EU financial coordination is a useful model for East Asia. The flexible EU approach is well suited to the Asian concept of regional cooperation. The "open coordination" method, involving self-control in peer groups, seems a suitable model in this regard for the near future. Such a method may sidestep the ingrained reluctance in the region to legalize regional links.

The agenda for intergovernmental financial cooperation in East Asia should contain four successive, or partly overlapping, phases.

PHASE ONE

The first phase (first 2 years) involves domestic authorities cooperating (through information exchange and a common indicative template) on postcrisis, or in-crisis, management, involving timely resolution of failed financial institutions (based on the principle of prompt corrective action). It is indeed astonishing that, while so many countries in the region are cleaning up the balance sheets of banks, for instance, through some form of asset management corporation, no common (even indicative) blueprint(s) and timetable(s) for this task has been agreed to or discussed at the regional level.

PHASE TWO

Regional financial cooperation in setting up regional countercyclical standards in prudential regulation—taking care of both expected and unexpected bank losses—is a priority, but comes only in the second phase (years 3–5). Adopting such standards, adapted to domestic needs and left to the discretion of national authorities, should be the stepping-stone toward eventual mutual recognition. Improving the effectiveness of banking regulation and supervision and ensuring the practical application of supervisory rules to all institutions that de facto engage in banking activities is also an essential component. Voluntary participation in the Financial Sector Assessment Program (FSAP) of the IMF-World Bank (IMF 2000) could be useful in giving clear signals to some countries about both the level of achievement and the tasks ahead. At the regional level, work should be started on financial soundness indicators (IMF 2001b) based on the capital, asset quality, management, earnings, and liquidity (CAMEL) framework, complementing the initiatives on macroeconomic indicators of external vulnerability.

PHASE THREE

The third step (over 5 years) includes regional minimum harmonization of a set of regulations, rules, etc. This will be complementary to the fields identified as suitable for mutual recognition, but will involve a much more demanding and time-consuming process. It should aim at ensuring competition and limiting the degree of direct or indirect government interference in the financial system.

Beyond 10 years, the next step is to build a stronger financial system (possibly giving more room for corporate bond finance) with full domestic financial liberalization. The longer term, but clearly defined, goal should be to build an Asian Financial Area. This last step involves full external financial liberalization at the regional level, which assumes that any remaining capital account restrictions have been lifted.

FORUMS

Key forums in the financial field should include an East Asian Banking Advisory Committee (EABAC) composed of high-level representatives of the 13 countries' supervisory authorities and finance ministries. The EABAC's role will be in phase two: (i) establish detailed proposals on common prudential standards at the regional/subregional level, and (ii) exchange information and discuss banking supervision issues of a domestic systemic character. This committee should meet four times a year.

Meetings of Banking Supervisors of East Asian countries (MBSEA) should gather mid-management banking supervisors involved in the day-to-day supervision of banks in the ASEAN+3 countries. The role of the MBSEA would be to (i) exchange information, in a purely confidential way, on individual banking cases relevant to banking supervision; and (ii) review developments in the different countries' supervisory systems, and prepare comparative reports on supervisory and regulatory issues, for instance regular (annual) reports on banking sector compliance with prudential and profitability requirements (CAMEL framework). MBSEA should meet three or four times a year. Similar fora for insurance and securities may also be set up.

A secretariat for ASEAN+3 needs to be established in phase two as an independent unit to help the EABAC design regional benchmarks for standards, rules, and regulations, and to report regularly on the progress made against the benchmarks.

Conclusion

There seems to be wide scope for regional monetary and financial cooperation in East Asia through information exchange and surveillance. There are gaps in surveillance and information exchange mechanisms developed at the global level, even if improvements have been noticeable over the last 5 years. These gaps can usefully be filled by regional initiatives. East Asian countries have not remained inactive in the face of this need. They have initiated efforts, which, given the very short track record, have produced promising results. However, these efforts stop short of fully capitalizing on the current favorable conditions for regional monetary and financial cooperation.

The possible fields of cooperation involved are diverse, as are the objectives to be pursued. The road to be followed should not replicate the path western Europe has taken over the last few decades. In Europe, exchange rate coordination came first—financial cooperation followed. The East Asian region may benefit from inverting the order of priorities. The highest priority should undoubtedly involve restructuring and improving the regulation and supervision of the financial sector in many—if not all—of the countries in the region. This study has presented a clear agenda to address this task, taking a step-by-step approach based on an "open coordination" method. This, given its flexibility and the voluntary nature of involvement by participating countries, seems well suited to a region in which interference in each other's domestic affairs is not a tradition. Imposed harmonization should not be the priority and would be kept to a minimum.

Such cooperation should be accompanied in its early phases by improved information exchange and transparency on macroeconomic issues, together with enhanced peer surveillance. When such cooperation has resulted in restructuring domestic financial systems and strengthening the regulatory-supervisory apparatus—in line with newly designed regional standards—and when mechanisms for regional macroeconomic surveillance are well advanced, it will be possible to start an enhanced process of regional liquidity provision with associated conditionality. Indeed, the infrastructure for such a process will then be available. Exchange rate coordination, with its more demanding associated information exchange and surveillance requirements, may, in the medium to long run, turn out to be the by-product of such a successful strategy of regional macroeconomic and financial cooperation.

ACKNOWLEDGMENTS

The author would like to thank Benoît Coeuré, Masahiro Kawai, Srinivasa Madhur, Pradumna B. Rana, and Alfred Steinherr, as well as the participants of the finalization workshop organized for the ADB Study on Monetary and Financial Cooperation in East Asia and held at ADB in July 2002, for their useful inputs.

References

Asian Development Bank Institute (ADBI). 2000. How to Avoid Another Capital Account Crisis? Technical Background Paper, ADB Institute, May.

Buiter, W., G. Corsetti, and N. Roubini. 1993. Excessive Deficits: Sense and Nonsense in the Treaty of Maastricht. *Economic Policy: A European Forum*, 8, April, pp. 57–100.

Chui, M., R. Morris, and G. Pineau. 2002. The European Experience with Monetary and Exchange Rate Cooperation: Potential Lessons for Asia? Seminar on Regional Economic, Financial and Monetary Cooperation: The European and Asian Experiences, European Central Bank, Frankfurt, April.

Crow, J., R. Arriazu, and N. Thygesen. 1999. External Evaluation of Surveillance Report. Part 2. In *External Evaluation of IMF Surveillance*. IMF, pp. 9–91.

Eichengreen, B. 2001. Hanging Together? On Monetary and Financial Cooperation in East Asia. Conference on East Asia after the Crisis, World Bank and the Kennedy School of Government, Cambridge, 2–3 October.

European Commission (EC). 1999. Financial Services: Building a Framework for Action. Communication of the Commission, European Commission.

———. 2000. Institutional Arrangements for the Regulation and Supervision of the Financial Sector. European Commission, Internal Market Directorate General, January.

———. 2001. Involving Experts in the Process of National Policy Convergence. White Paper on Governance, Workshop no. 4, Consistency and Cooperation in a Networking Europe. June.

Gros, D., and N. Thygesen. 1998. *European Monetary Integration*. 2nd edition. London: Longman.

International Monetary Fund (IMF). 2000. Financial Sector Assessment Program, A Review: Lessons from the Pilot and Issues Going Forward, IMF-World Bank, Washington DC, November.

———. 2001a. Conditionality in Fund-Supported Programs: Policy Issues, Policy Development and Review Department, Washington, DC, February.

———. 2001b. Assessing the Implementation of Standards: An IMF Review of Experience and Next Steps. IMF Public Information Notice, 01/07, March.

Ito, T. 2002a. Regional Surveillance Mechanisms in East Asia. In Institute of Monetary Affairs, Report on the Study Group on Strengthening Financial Cooperation and Surveillance: Kobe Research Project, Tokyo, February, pp. 110–134.

———. 2002b. Exchange Rate Regimes for East Asia. Seminar on Regional Economic, Financial and Monetary Cooperation: The European and Asian Experiences, European Central Bank (ECB), Frankfurt, April.

Kahler, M. 2000. Legalization as Strategy: The Asia-Pacific Case. *International Organization* 54 (3, Summer): 549–571.

Kawai, M., and S. Takagi. 2000. Proposed Strategy for a Regional Exchange Rate Arrangement in Post-Crisis East Asia. World Bank, Policy Research Working Paper, no. 2503, December.

Kenen, P. B. 2000. Financial Reform in Emerging Market Countries: Getting the Incentives Right, Princeton University, June. (mimeo.)

Kuroda, H., and M. Kawai. 2002. Strengthening Regional Financial Cooperation in East Asia. Seminar on Regional Economic, Financial and Monetary Cooperation: The European and Asian Experiences, ECB, Frankfurt, April.

Kydd, A. 2000. Trust, Reassurance and Cooperation. *International Organization* 54(2): 325–357.

Lamberte, M. B. 2001. Reforming the International Financial Architecture: The East Asian View. In *Regional Financial Arrangements in East Asia*, edited by Y. H. Kim and Y. Wang, 123–164. Korea Institute for International Economic Policy.

Lamberte, M. B., M. M. S. Milo, and V. Pontines. 2001. Enhancing Economic Integration in East Asia through Closer Monetary Cooperation. Philippine Institute for Development Studies, Discussion Paper no. 2001–16, July.

Manzano, G. 2001. Is There Any Value-Added in the ASEAN Surveillance Process? Center for International Economic Studies, University of Adelaide, Discussion Paper no. 0105, February.

Rajan, R. 1999. Financial and Macroeconomic Cooperation in ASEAN: Issues and Policy Initiatives. University of Adelaide, Center for International Economic Studies, Working Paper, no. 99/29, December.

———. 2000. Examining the Case for an Asian Monetary Fund. University of Adelaide, Center for International Economic Studies, Working Paper no. 00/02, January.

Rana, P. 2002. Monetary and Financial Cooperation in East Asia and the Establishment of an Early Warning System: A Review. Seminar on Regional Economic, Financial and Monetary Cooperation: The European and Asian Experiences, ECB, Frankfurt, April.

Tetsuji, M. 2002. Regional Surveillance and Policy Coordination: Experience of Europe and Lessons for East Asia. In Institute of Monetary Affairs, Report on the Study Group on Strengthening Financial Cooperation and Surveillance, 41–73. Kobe Research Project, Tokyo, February.

Tsoukalis, L. 1997. *The New European Economy Revisited.* Oxford: Oxford University Press.

United Nations Economic and Social Commission for Asia and Pacific (UN ESCAP). 2001. Monitoring and Surveillance: The Theoretical Underpinnings. In ESCAP, *Economic and Social Survey of Asia and the Pacific,* pp. 151–248.

Wyplosz, C. 1998a. International Financial Instability. Graduate Institute for International Studies, Geneva, July.

———. 1998b. Speculative Attacks and Capital Mobility. Graduate Institute for International Studies, Geneva, July.

———. 1998c. Globalized Financial Markets and Financial Crises. Graduate Institute for International Studies, Geneva, April.

———. 2001. A Monetary Union in Asia? Some European Lessons. Graduate Institute for International Studies, Geneva.

Yoshitomi, M., and S. Shirai. 2000. Policy Recommendations for Preventing Another Capital Account Crisis. Technical Background Paper, ADB Institute, July.

3 Reserve pooling in East Asia: beyond the Chiang Mai Initiative

OLARN CHAIPRAVAT

Following the 1997–1998 Asian financial crisis, there has been intensified interest within the region in increased economic cooperation. Macroeconomic cooperation can take different forms: information sharing and surveillance, liquidity provision, and exchange rate coordination. Of these, progress within the region has been most evident in liquidity provision. Following the adoption of the Chiang Mai initiative (CMI) and the associated multilateral intra-Association of Southeast Asian Nations (ASEAN) currency swap agreement among the ASEAN+3 countries,[1] a series of bilateral currency swap agreements had already been formalized. This study will consider the question of what further progress can and should be made on this front in the East Asian region, both in the near future and over the medium term.

At present, the ASEAN+3 swap arrangements are subject to the limitation that 90% of the available resources can be drawn only on condition that the borrowing country has carried out an adjustment program supported by the International Monetary Fund (IMF). A key issue to be considered in this study for the

[1] ASEAN+3 consists of ASEAN's 10 member countries—Brunei Darussalam, Cambodia, Indonesia, Lao People's Democratic Republic, Malaysia, Myanmar, Philippines, Singapore, Thailand, and Viet Nam—plus People's Republic of China, Japan, and Republic of Korea.

short and medium term, therefore, is whether these arrangements should be delinked from a country's participation in an IMF-supported adjustment program and, if so, under what alternative conditions those resources should be made available. In particular, should an expanded set of conditions—different from the "traditional" IMF norms—be designed for ASEAN+3 swap arrangements that may be more suitable for confronting the type of "capital account-induced" instability that characterized the 1997–1998 crisis?

A logical follow-up question is whether the CMI should eventually be superseded by more ambitious regional arrangements for liquidity provision, i.e., can the financial authorities of developing East Asian countries pool enough financial resources to effectively counteract any speculative attacks that might be faced in the future? If so, how should such a resource pool be administered? Should it be centralized or decentralized in structure? And what are the conditions, both ex ante and ex post, that will minimize the risk of moral hazard and assure that resources are used for legitimate purposes and are then repaid after the crisis is averted or successfully resolved?

Looking into the longer term, if ASEAN+3 countries (except Japan) adopt a regional exchange rate arrangement, what type of resource pooling and resource provision arrangements would be most effective in defending the coordinated currency peg regimes? What are the relative sizes of the pooled financial resource requirements for the leading alternatives among possible regimes—e.g., a hard peg (100%) against a single major currency (e.g., the United States [US] dollar), or a triangular basket peg against three major currencies (US dollar, yen, and euro)?

Last, what type of collective secretariat institution would be required to support enhanced regional reserve-sharing arrangements? What would be the politically acceptable institutional setup, for example, for monitoring the origins of shocks and giving technical advice to the political leaderships of member countries? If the origins of instability can generally be identified clearly and accepted by all members, is it still necessary to set up a large regional secretariat for financial resource pooling, information monitoring, and surveillance? Or would a small secretariat to oversee the networking of individual country monitoring and surveillance suffice?

This study will attempt to address these issues. Based on the experiences of many East Asian countries before and after the 1997 crisis as well as on the reaction of financial authorities—including the formation of ASEAN+3, the CMI, ongoing discussions at the regional level from leadership summit meetings down to technical cooperation and joint studies—it appears that there is sufficient political and technical consensus in the region to proceed proactively in all these areas. As data and experience are further accumulated, the collective political leadership can take a series of concrete actions. It is hoped that this study will provide another stone in the path toward a new ASEAN+3 financial infrastructure and perhaps, in the more distant future, toward a common currency area and full integration of trade and investment in East Asia.

The structure of this paper is as follows: since the focus is on regional arrangements for liquidity provision, a natural starting point is a discussion of the CMI and the conditions under which the conditionality attached to drawings from regional swap arrangements can be modified. After that discussion, two proposals for extending regional liquidity provision beyond the existing swap arrangements are described. Since the need for doing so is in part related to the exchange rate regimes maintained by the participating countries, the relationship between enhancements in regional liquidity-provision arrangements and potential future regional exchange coordination is examined. New institutional arrangements that would be conducive to furthering regional mechanisms for liquidity provision are considered next. Two subsequent sections describe a concrete action plan for the region, including motivations for the action plan, and a proposed timetable. The final section gives a summing up and conclusions.

The Chiang Mai Initiative and associated swap arrangements

The CMI arose out of a meeting of ASEAN+3 finance ministers and central bank governors held on the sidelines of the Asian

Development Bank (ADB) Board of Governors Annual Meeting in Chiang Mai, Thailand, in May 2000. The CMI was intended to provide financial assistance to countries in the region through a series of multilateral and bilateral currency swap arrangements under which any member country can theoretically borrow hard currency from the other signatories in times of financial distress. Some bilateral swap agreements, e.g., that between the People's Republic of China (PRC) and Japan, do not involve the US dollar but only the currencies of the two signatories, i.e., they are "soft" or "nonmajor" currencies. Significantly, a condition attached to the standard bilateral agreements is that to utilize more than 10% of the agreed swap lines (say, of $3 billion equivalent), the borrowing country must enter into an IMF-supported program first.

Given the dissatisfaction in the region with the speed of disbursement of IMF funds and the conditions attached to IMF lending, this raises the question of whether there are alternative and superior forms of conditionality that would address the problem of moral hazard associated with the activation of the swaps.

Many analysts concluded that the major source of financial instability during the 1997–1998 Asian financial crisis, as manifested in Asian currencies' rapid depreciation against the US dollar, was volatile short-term portfolio capital inflows and outflows induced by global fund managers ("hot money"), rather than the relatively predictable "fundamental" export/import trade flows or long-term foreign direct investment flows (see, for example, Yoshitomi and Shirai [2000]).[2] This interpretation of the role of "hot money" flows is widely held within the region. Thus, in considering alternative conditionality, it must be kept in mind that *the objective of regional financial swap agreements in East Asia has been both to prevent and to react to the extreme exchange rate instabilities caused by disruptive short-term portfolio capital inflows and outflows.*

One implication of this objective is that countries that are potential lenders in regional swap arrangements will have an interest in determining the extent to which the need for resources

[2] Masaru Yoshitomi and Sayuri Shirai. 2000. Policy Recommendations for Preventing Another Capital Account Crisis. *ADB Institute Working Paper Series*, Tokyo, July.

by potential borrowers in such arrangements has been caused by the effects of volatile exogenous flows. Thus, unless and until countries in the region are able to monitor these short-term inflows and outflows with sufficient accuracy to identify their role in the emergence of instability, potential lenders will not feel comfortable with their obligations under swap arrangements. While they may be willing to provide resources in response to shocks arising from exogenous changes in the disposition of "hot money," they will be reluctant to do so in response to internally generated imbalances for fear that borrowing countries will misuse the resources provided. To part from or improve upon IMF conditions, this fear must be squarely acknowledged and properly addressed, rather than left understood but not articulated clearly.

The implication is that the first ex ante condition for a departure from IMF conditionality must be that each member country's financial authority develops an effective capital account monitoring system capable of identifying and distinguishing short-term portfolio inflows/outflows from desirable long-term capital flows on a weekly or monthly basis. Without some legal framework for exchange control procedures, no matter how limited, as practiced in most ASEAN countries (such as Malaysia, Singapore, and Thailand from 1950 to the mid-1990s), it would be difficult to monitor short-term capital movements through banking and capital market registrations and reports. The original purpose of these registrations is to facilitate repatriations of capital for foreign portfolio investors. By the early 1990s, many countries were already abolishing or planning to abolish these reports under the new wave of full capital account liberalization (e.g., Indonesia, Republic of Korea [Korea], and Philippines). In light of the aforementioned reason, *it is advisable for newer members of ASEAN, such as Cambodia, Lao People's Democratic Republic, Myanmar, and Viet Nam to bring in this reporting system and, for those that no longer possess it, to reinstate some form of reporting either through banking or stock/bond market registrations.*

Malaysia and Thailand still have a reporting system of this type that can be studied and replicated by other developing East and Southeast Asian countries, even though their stock markets may not yet appear on the radar screen of global portfolio investors.

Even for Japan, whose currency is already internationalized, this report should also be compiled in the same manner as carried out by the US Treasury, which publishes its report on foreigners' portfolio transactions in its monthly statistical release.[3]

A careful monitoring of capital flows is the first condition for the departure from a link to IMF conditionality in regional swap arrangements. A second condition is designed to protect countries in the region from the effects of such flows, thereby reducing the magnitude of "hot money" shocks. It involves the imposition of *limitations on residents' holdings of financial assets and liabilities denominated in foreign currencies and nonresidents' holdings of similar instruments denominated in the local currency*. A set of rules to this effect must be spelled out clearly and enforced by the financial authorities. Malaysia and Singapore have the most detailed systems of this type, and these can be modified to suit other countries' requirements—so long, of course, as the full internationalization of the local currency is not an immediate objective. The effects of such conditions would be to diminish the size of the shocks to which drawings on swap lines would be intended to respond.

A third condition is a *step-by-step program to regionalize domestic currencies*. This will serve as a useful starting point for the final internationalization of the currency. Unless and until a regional clearing system is established, even the use of regional currencies as a medium of exchange cannot be realized. The use of these currencies as a store of value can follow quickly if capital flow restrictions allow for some international capital transactions *among nations in East Asia*. If equities and bonds are to be traded across countries, stock markets and securities and exchange commissions must also be brought in, to develop international settlement/clearing systems for these financial instruments.

Once all these conditions are met and full monitoring in each country is possible, it will become easier for a small regional secretariat to oversee the free flow of information across countries and to identify major sources of instabilities in foreign exchange markets when they arise. If it is monitored and confirmed that

[3] See Table CM-V-4. *US Treasury Bulletin*, 2002. US Government Printing Office, March.

exchange rate fluctuations are caused by disruptive short-term capital flows, the use of pooled financial resources can be activated quickly without linking such use to the activation of an IMF-supported program.

In short, what is proposed is the use of regional swap facilities in a lender-of-last-resort role in a context in which the region's financial links with the rest of the world are weakened. Such facilities would be available regionally to confront liquidity crises, rather than solvency problems. It is clear that if instabilities are caused by fundamental disequilibria in the current account as a result of overexpansionary fiscal policy or cost-push domestic inflation, for example, this pooled resource would not be activated without policy conditionality. In the latter case, use of the pooled resource would be subject to realignment of the currency values and other IMF-style policy adjustments before the newly aligned currency peg is defended again (see the section Institutional Setup and Political Feasibilities for an ASEAN+3 Secretariat).

Resource pooling and borrowing entitlements for ASEAN+3[4]

The CMI was a landmark in the formal institutionalization of coherent monetary and financial cooperation among the participating regional member countries. As a starting point, multilateralism was officially instituted among the 10 ASEAN member countries in the form of an ASEAN swap arrangement (ASA). The principles of the ASA are a significant step forward, but the scale of the facility still falls short of what would be required to combat or at least discourage speculative attacks on a regional currency. The ASEAN arrangement to borrow, on the other hand, has not proven its usefulness, while the ASEAN bilateral repurchase agreement (Repo) is a financing facility that has never thus far been resorted to by any ASEAN member country. Thus, *it is essential that sufficiently*

[4] Based on Bhasu Bhanich Supapol. 2002. Regional Resource Provision Arrangements for Enhanced Monetary and Financial Cooperation in East Asia: The Chiang Mai Initiative and Beyond. Prepared for the Asian Development Bank.

large facilities be arranged and made available for just-in-time disbursements, with proper ex ante and ex post conditions established to combat moral hazard.

The bilateral swap arrangement (BSA) within the ASEAN+3 framework adds to the above financial support. What is crucial, however, is that the BSA brings with it the direct participation of the three Northeast Asian countries. Without their involvement, the intra-ASEAN self-help and support mechanisms would be rather negligible. Equally significant, as part of the welcome new mind-set with regard to the BSA, is the introduction and acceptance of the use of local currencies in resource provision and sharing. As increasing numbers of BSAs are concluded, a web of bilateral cooperation is being spun that may eventually cover the entire region in a network of effective monetary and financial cooperation. *These driving concepts—multilateralization of the process, Northeast Asian direct participation, and use of local currencies—can form the basis for a future decentralized regional reserve pooling arrangement that can materially add to the resources available under the aegis of the CMI.*

A specific proposal for such an arrangement is based on the observation that, both under current conditions and in the event that some form of regional exchange rate coordination is adopted in the future, regional central banks will continue to intervene in the foreign exchange market. A multilateral reserve pooling arrangement can be based on the disposition of new foreign exchange reserves accumulated from short-term capital inflows (identified as such under the procedures described in the last section).

To be concrete, as foreign exchange from such sources accumulates in the reserve account of a central bank, a specified portion—say 60%—of the increase in reserves could remain independently managed by the central bank. However, the remaining portion (40%) would be placed as deposits with the other member central banks in some equitable and mutually acceptable formula, e.g., on the basis of the outstanding international reserves of these countries. Under current conditions, Japan and the PRC would take up most of the new deposits, as they have the largest and the second largest reserves among the ASEAN+3 countries, respectively. All participating members would have to abide by the same rules both as suppliers (60:40 basis) and recipients (reserves size basis) of these intercountry deposits. Once the definition and measurement of the central bank's intervention amount arising from short-term capital inflows are agreed upon and implemented collectively by member countries, intercountry placements of deposits would continue to increase so long as short-term capital flows into the region persisted. Table 3.1 shows the hypothetical increase in international reserves for a sustained period, say 12 months, of short-term capital flows into Thailand. The Appendix contains corresponding tables for other ASEAN+3 countries.

By the end of an initial 12-month period, the accumulated "windfall" for Thailand would hypothetically amount to about \$1.29 billion, \$772 million or 60% of which would be managed independently by the Thai central bank, while \$515 million would be out-placed as deposits with other member central banks. These deposit recipients would be permitted to manage these placements in whatever way they see fit, but the reserve assets would have to be liquid in case they are needed to honor lending obligations as stipulated in the swap and related agreements. Once short-term capital flow reversals occur, each central bank can use its own-managed 60% of accumulated reserves to intervene in the foreign exchange market to defend its currency. If that is not enough, the central bank could automatically draw on the accumulated 40% portion from the recipient central banks.

The next tranche of funds would represent true intercountry assistance arrangements, whereby the requesting country can borrow from its partners up to the amount of total swap lines available (e.g., the equivalent of \$5 billion in the case of Thailand) as stipulated in bilateral or multilateral currency swap agreements (Tables 3.2 and 3.3).[5] So long as it is confirmed that exchange rate instabilities are caused by short-term capital outflows and the central bank in question needs to sell hard currencies to

[5] Illustrative tables for other East Asian countries, with the exception of the new members of ASEAN, are presented in the Appendix for brevity. These smaller countries can be included in the scheme without any problem.

Table 3.1 **Thailand's Hypothetical Exchange Rate, and Short-Term Reserve Accumulation and Management**

Period	Average Exchange Rate			Average SET Index	Thailand's Excess Short-Term Reserve Accumulation ($ million equivalent)		
	Yen/$	Euro/$	Baht/$		Central Bank $ Purchase (+) from Short-Term Capital Inflows	Managed by Own Central Bank (60%)	Placed With Other Central Banks (40%)
Jan 02	132.94	1.1578	44.04	340.82	103	62	41
Feb 02	133.89	1.1559	43.85	371.81	128	77	51
Mar 02	132.71	1.1463	43.42	373.95	88	53	35
Apr 02	127.97	1.1101	43.44	371.42	68	41	27
May 02	123.96	1.0929	42.79	407.96	200	120	80
Jun 02	122.00	1.0756	42.49	420.00	100	60	40
Jul 02	120.00	1.0580	42.18	432.00	100	60	40
Aug 02	118.00	1.0403	41.87	444.00	100	60	40
Sep 02	116.00	1.0227	41.56	456.00	100	60	40
Oct 02	114.00	1.0051	41.25	468.00	100	60	40
Nov 02	112.00	0.9874	40.94	480.00	100	60	40
Dec 02	110.00	0.9698	40.63	492.00	100	60	40
Jan 03	111.00	0.9786	40.78	480.00	-100	0	0
Feb 03	112.00	0.9874	40.94	460.00	-200	0	0
Mar 03	113.00	0.9962	41.09	440.00	-200	0	0
Apr 03	114.00	1.0051	41.25	420.00	-200	0	0
May 03	115.00	1.0139	41.40	400.00	-200	0	0
Jun 03	116.00	1.0227	41.56	380.00	-200	0	0
Jul 03	117.00	1.0315	41.71	360.00	-200	0	0
Aug 03	118.00	1.0403	41.87	340.00	-200	0	0
Sep 03	119.00	1.0491	42.02	320.00	-200	0	0
Oct 03	120.00	1.0580	42.18	300.00	-200	0	0
Nov 03	121.00	1.0668	42.33	280.00	-200	0	0
Dec 03	122.00	1.0756	42.49	260.00	-200	0	0

Note: Data from Jan 02 to May 02 are actual. For Jun 02 and after, data are estimates and for illustration only.
Source: Stock Exchange of Thailand (SET).

defend its currency peg, the additional tranche of funds could be drawn down automatically without the condition that the country enters into the IMF program first. Table 3.4 shows hypothetical borrowings under these two lines of defense for Thailand's central bank in the event that it needs hard currencies to defend its currency peg regime up to the total swap lines with other countries.

Table 3.2 **Bank of Thailand Out-Placements with Other Central Banks as a Result of Excessive Short-Term Capital Inflows Absorbed by the Central Bank** ($ million)

Period	Japan	People's Republic of China	Republic of Korea	Singapore	Malaysia	Indonesia	Philippines	Total for Thailand
Jan 02	19.20	10.14	4.91	3.62	1.47	1.34	0.54	41.23
Feb 02	23.76	12.54	6.08	4.48	1.82	1.66	0.67	51.02
Mar 02	16.45	8.68	4.21	3.10	1.26	1.15	0.47	35.32
Apr 02	12.76	6.73	3.26	2.41	0.98	0.89	0.36	27.39
May 02	37.26	19.67	9.53	7.03	2.86	2.60	1.06	80.00
Jun 02	18.63	9.83	4.77	3.51	1.43	1.30	0.53	40.00
Jul 02	18.63	9.83	4.77	3.51	1.43	1.30	0.53	40.00
Aug 02	18.63	9.83	4.77	3.51	1.43	1.30	0.53	40.00
Sep 02	18.63	9.83	4.77	3.51	1.43	1.30	0.53	40.00
Oct 02	18.63	9.83	4.77	3.51	1.43	1.30	0.53	40.00
Nov 02	18.63	9.83	4.77	3.51	1.43	1.30	0.53	40.00
Dec 02	18.63	9.83	4.77	3.51	1.43	1.30	0.53	40.00
Total[a]	239.85	126.60	61.35	45.23	18.41	16.72	6.80	514.96

Note: Assuming that all agreements as proposed in this study have been in place since January 2002 and that Thailand's currency swap agreements with the People's Republic of China, Japan, and Republic of Korea have been modified to reflect this study's conditionalities, and not those of the International Monetary Fund (IMF).
[a] Total Thailand out-placements by country.

Table 3.3 **International Reserve by Country and Proportion at End-December 2001, to Be Used by the Bank of Thailand for Depositing Out-Placements**

Item	Japan	People's Republic of China	Republic of Korea	Singapore	Malaysia	Indonesia	Philippines	Total for Thailand
International reserve ($ million)	401,959	212,165	102,821	75,800	30,848	28,016	11,391	863,000
Proportion	0.47	0.25	0.12	0.09	0.04	0.03	0.01	1.00

Source: IMF, *International Financial Statistics*.

The achievement of resource pooling and sharing in the form presented above relies heavily on the potential success of the multilateralization process. The proposed multilateralization is expected to proceed in a similar fashion as the multilateral arrangement among the 10 ASEAN member countries conceived

Table 3.4 **Thailand's Hypothetical Accumulation of Excess Short-Term Reserves, Reversal, and Financing** ($ million)

	Thailand Operations			
		Central Bank Intervention		
Period	Central Bank Purchase (+) from Short-Term Capital Inflows	Using Excess Short-Term Reserves Placed at Own Central Bank (60%)	Using Excess Short-Term Reserves Placed with Other Central Banks (40%)	Using Bilateral Swap Agreements
Jan 02	103	0	0	0
Feb 02	128	0	0	0
Mar 02	88	0	0	0
Apr 02	68	0	0	0
May 02	200	0	0	0
Jun 02	100	0	0	0
Jul 02	100	0	0	0
Aug 02	100	0	0	0
Sep 02	100	0	0	0
Oct 02	100	0	0	0
Nov 02	100	0	0	0
Dec 02	100	0	0	0
Jan 03	-100	100	0	0
Feb 03	-200	200	0	0
Mar 03	-200	200	0	0
Apr 03	-200	200	0	0
May 03	-200	72	128	0
Jun 03	-200	0	200	0
Jul 03	-200	0	187	13
Aug 03	-200	0	0	200
Sep 03	-200	0	0	200
Oct 03	-200	0	0	200
Nov 03	-200	0	0	200
Dec 03	-200	0	0	200

Note: Data from Jun 02 and after are for illustration only.
Source: Stock Exchange of Thailand.

in Bandar Seri Begawan, Brunei Darussalam, in late 2000. A unique feature of the proposed regional financial arrangement is that it represents a pooled, yet decentralized, system of resource provision. The envisaged multilateral facility under the proposed mechanism would, as a by-product, enable certain member countries to obtain financing from the Northeast Asian countries to which otherwise they might not be able to gain access under a limited bilateral framework.

The preceding proposal approaches cooperative arrangement from both the asset side (i.e., international reserves) and the liability side (i.e., borrowings) of the 13 monetary authorities. The proposal introduces the concept of "constructive engagement," whereby the participating monetary authorities would be acquainted with the modalities and mechanisms of the arrangement through active participation and a committed relationship among the participants well ahead of the time of actual financial need. All participants would then be in a position to deal with an emergency situation without delay. The arrangement is also based on the principle of give and take, which in itself ensures a certain degree of equity and fairness as well as provides a logical foundation for a system of financial self-help and support in the region.

The proposed multilateral reserve-sharing arrangement just described would not represent a net addition to the resources available to any participating country for exchange market intervention, however, if countries were only able to make use of their own deposits with other central banks. The gain in liquidity arises from the availability of deposits provided by other central banks as reserves. This gain is, of course, zero for the region as a whole, but it will tend to be positive for smaller countries in the region, which will receive deposits from large countries that exceed in magnitude their own out-placements. Thus, the scheme essentially involves a redistribution of reserves from larger countries in Northeast Asia to smaller ones in Southeast Asia. In effect, it makes financial assistance from large-reserve countries to small-reserve countries automatic.

In some instances, however, a country may need more than the resources it has itself generated, its deposits from other regional central banks, and its combined existing borrowing lines to defend its currency peg. To cope with such circumstances, a third tranche of resources could be made available. This tranche could take one of two forms, depending on whether countries in the region prefer to continue to work under a decentralized, multilateral design for future regional liquidity provision or whether more centralized arrangements become feasible within the region.

If a decentralized arrangement is retained, then the size of existing swap lines could be enlarged, under the condition that the expanded lines be drawn upon only to counter documented "hot money" outflows. In effect, this would simply increase the volume of resources available under "second tranche" conditions. Under this arrangement, as under the present ones, the ultimate decision to activate a swap line would remain with the lending country, which would retain the responsibility for monitoring the uses to which resources are put by the borrowing country.

The alternative is a more centralized reserve-pooling arrangement. Such an arrangement could take various forms. Their common feature, however, is that the ultimate decision concerning the disbursement of resources as well as the monitoring of their use would rest with a central regional reserve-disbursing authority, which would presumably be administered by representatives of the participating countries. Such a centralized arrangement could build on the multilateral cross-deposit proposal described above. For example, countries could be entitled to draw some *multiple* of their own deposits with other regional central banks from the regional reserve pool. These drawings would be funded from the reserves of other regional central banks in proportions that are prorated to their own contributions to intraregional reserve deposits.

The size of the reserve pool and regional exchange rate arrangements

Under either of these medium-term arrangements, the resources available to each individual participating country could exceed what is currently available from own funds, other central banks' deposits, and existing swaps by whatever amount regional authorities find appropriate. It is worth noting, however, that the optimal size of the reserve pool is likely to depend on the exchange rate arrangements prevailing within the region at the time that the decision concerning the size of the reserve pool is made. For now, proposals for regional exchange rate coordination focus on two alternatives: a common single-currency peg and a common basket peg.

The amount of intervention that a developing country with reasonably diversified trade and financial relationships (as is the case with most economies in East Asia) will have to undertake under these alternatives—and, thus, its need for foreign exchange resources—will obviously be influenced by cross movements among the major currencies. Pegging to a single currency will call for more extensive intervention in the foreign exchange market if that currency exhibits sharp movements against those of the country's other trading partners.

Recently, international portfolio investors seem to have exhibited a bipolar world view, treating US dollar assets as a distinct class relative to the rest of the world's asset classes. This has resulted in the values of the yen and euro moving together while the dollar has moved in the opposite direction (the yen/dollar exchange rate movement over time having a strong positive covariance with that of the euro/dollar exchange rate). Figure 3.1 shows the strong positive relationship between daily yen/dollar and euro/dollar exchange rate indexes. The correlation coefficient (r) for the last 3.5 years (January 1999–May 2002) is as high as 0.87. The assumption of the bipolar worldview of international portfolio investors thus seems to be supported by empirical evidence. This view is supported further by the fact that, for the same period, the correlation coefficient (r) between yen/dollar and baht/dollar exchange rate indexes is also positive and high at 0.88.

Under these conditions, the amount of financial resources needed by the financial authorities to intervene successfully to keep the target exchange rate within reasonable bands will tend to be less under the triangular basket peg than under the hard peg to the US dollar alone. In the case of Thailand, for example, the relative size of the resources needed under the triangular basket peg would be about one half of what would be required under the hard peg regime (100% US dollar), if data from January to May 2002 are analyzed. If data on short-term portfolio capital inflows and outflows are available, a similar calculation can be performed for other developing countries of ASEAN+3. Moreover, as long as countries' trade and financial relationships with the

Figure 3.1 **Daily Exchange Rates of Yen/Dollar and Euro/Dollar, January–May 2002**

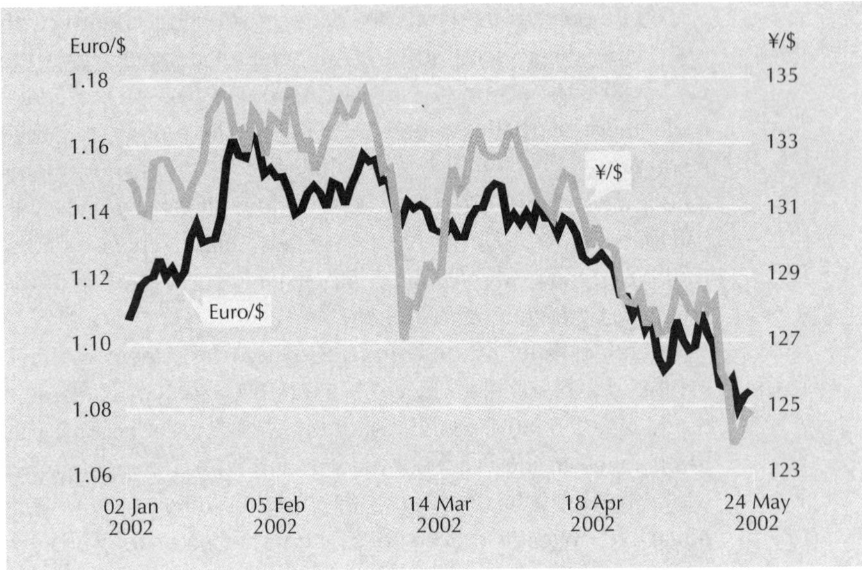

Source: CEIC Data Co., Ltd.

major-currency countries remain fairly diversified, it will generally be true that even if the international portfolio investors' worldview is not bipolar in the future, i.e., even if a strong negative covariance between the yen/dollar and euro/dollar exchange rate time series emerges, the triangular basket peg will still require less intervention, and therefore smaller foreign exchange resources, than the hard peg.

Institutional setup and political feasibilities for an ASEAN+3 secretariat[6]

The proposals offered in the section Resource Pooling and Borrowing Entitlements for ASEAN+3 have one thing in common:

[6] Based on Kanit Sangsubhan. 2002. Political and Institutional Setting for Effective Financial Resource Sharing and Cooperation in East Asia. Prepared for the Asian Development Bank.

both are capable of generating a significant increase in the liquid resources available to individual countries of East Asia. The key difference between the two proposals concerns their institutional requirements. Under the first proposal, the out-placements from excessive short-term capital inflows and borrowing entitlements to defend regional currencies are decentralized in nature. Also, the system does not require any centralized secretariat so long as the conditions and rules are clearly articulated and mutually agreed upon by the ASEAN+3 countries. The second proposal, however, featuring a system of centralized resource pooling, obviously calls for substantially more regional institution-building. There is, therefore, an issue as to how countries in the region can proceed from the present state of case-by-case cooperative agreements to a system of centralized resource pooling and an institutional setup for monitoring, surveillance, policy making, and implementation of major initiatives by the ASEAN+3 governments. This section highlights some ways to move forward in designing politically acceptable institutional transitions.

The success of cross-border economic and financial cooperation will depend on whether the required institutions are set up properly, on how well they represent the group's interests and reflect the group's sentiments, on how competently they provide the required technical support, and on whether they can draw enough participation from inside and outside the region. The issue relating to effective technical support is particularly worth emphasizing at this rather early stage of development of regional liquidity-provision mechanisms. While it may be sufficient to have a technical group of people in the simple form of expert networking at first, the later stages of development in regional cooperation will require the setting up of a permanent technical group within the institution's perimeters.

Some progress has already been made in this area, and the need for further deepening the regional surveillance process has already been recognized. Following the formulation of the ASEAN Financial Work Program, there has been closer consultation on economic policy matters via the ASEAN Surveillance Process. The ASEAN Surveillance Coordination Unit (ASCU) works in coordination with the assigned country surveillance units and in close consultation with the Regional Economic Monitoring Unit (REMU) of ADB and regional offices of IMF. Recently, a request to establish a new financial unit in the ASCU was approved by the ASEAN Finance Ministers' Meeting (AFMM) in Yangon, Myanmar.

Looking forward, ASEAN Vision 2020 together with the Surveillance Process will be essential for an ASEAN monitoring and warning system. *A system of monitoring, surveillance, and peer review must be incorporated into and made an integral part of any regional liquidity-provision scheme.* In addition, *political and institutional arrangements for joint deliberation and decision making must be put in place* to conduct the required information gathering, analysis, and setting up of conditions to carry out the ensuing operations for the entire East Asian region. In this regard, *a monitoring and surveillance unit must be established to screen and make recommendations upon the request of member countries in times of shortage of international financial resources.* The unit must also be in a position to give early warnings to such countries before a crisis emerges. Moreover, if regional liquidity provision is extended to objectives beyond countering "hot money" flows, problems of moral hazard could be avoided by bringing fiscal and monetary discipline to the member countries through a surveillance process.

To tackle the problem on a region-wide basis, the required institution should consist of a group of reliable and competent people who are authorized to oversee policies that are agreed upon by the participating countries in a cooperative arrangement. The institution would also take the lead in preparing the next suggested policy moves and in paving the way for an effective decision-making process. The envisioned resource provision to prevent a recurrence of another Asian economic and financial crisis may be severely impaired by moral hazard if the liquidity-provision arrangement is not equipped with an appropriate institution to properly perform the necessary functions. The institution will therefore need continued enhancement of its intellectual capacity.

To this end, a joint paper of Bank Negara Malaysia and Japan's Ministry of Finance presented at the AFMM in April 2002 suggested the setting up of an Eminent Persons Group (EPG). This part of the paper did not, however, receive approval and will have to be considered again in the next ASEAN Finance and Central Bank Deputies Meeting (AFDM+3). This study supports any effort to reinforce institutional capacity in the region, but would suggest as well the establishment of a permanent "Technical Forum" to work hand in hand with the EPG. To strengthen the intellectual capacity of an ASEAN+3 secretariat with purely technical analyses and nonbinding assessments, it may be preferable to have an independent academic network or forum to provide support through technical studies and policy suggestions. The studies and suggestions would be first reviewed by the EPG and later deliberated on by the AFDM+3 and AFMM+3 for final decisions and actions.

This intellectual forum might be named the East Asian Regional Financial Arrangement (EARFA) Forum. It would be composed of policy research institutes or top policy researchers of the ASEAN+3 member countries. The EARFA Forum would have to reidentify the types of technical support that it should provide to sub-groupings within ASEAN+3, as their needs may vary. It should work toward fulfilling the needs of member countries where existing institutions may not be in an optimal position to do so.

Motivations for a recommended action plan for East Asia

A relatively large and up-front financial resource pool among the ASEAN+3 countries is essential for the success of any future regional arrangement for liquidity provision. But some potential lending countries with large international reserves will be reluctant to participate in centralized reserve pooling on day one, for various reasons. These could include a fear of the moral hazard problem, inadequate monitoring and surveillance processes, conditions that are not strong enough or may be perceived as not suitable within the region's economic and financial context, or because of a perceived inadequacy of repayment mechanisms for short-term borrowed funds.

To address these justifiable concerns, a step-by-step engagement process that is constructive in nature may be required for member countries. This "constructive engagement" process, if undertaken over the next 5–15 years, will help allay or reduce some apprehensions and worries so that the spirit of cooperation can be turned into a series of actual engagements and interactions that are beneficial to all ASEAN+3 countries.

First, to address and reduce these fears, potential borrowing countries must be willing to show that the relationship would not constitute a one-way street, but would in fact be of a two-way, give-and-take nature. Under the multilateral arrangement proposed in the preceding section, the more vulnerable countries can build up goodwill and demonstrate this conviction by setting aside portions of their excessive international reserve increases gained from short-term portfolio capital inflows and depositing them with other monetary authorities in the region. This would show that during "good times" the resource could willingly be shared.

Recent history can help illustrate this possibility. Imagine Indonesia, Korea, Malaysia, and Thailand setting aside portions of their large international reserve increases arising out of short-term portfolio capital inflows and placing them with the PRC and Japan during the "boom years" from 1987 to 1995. Almost 10 years of financial resource pooling would have built up a sizable pool of reserves—information that would have been known to all outsiders. If it is also known that this pooled resource (along with international reserves of the region's richest countries) can be used to defend chosen currency regimes when massive short-term portfolio capital flow reversals occur, attacks on even the weakest country by outside manipulative speculators[7] might be deterred.

---

[7] Without any moral or ethical connotation, we distinguish between "speculators" and "manipulators" in the same way that Joseph Yam, Chief Executive of the Hong Kong Monetary Authority, did in a speech in Tokyo on 12 July 2002. "Speculators" try to buy low now and sell high later or to sell high now with the expectation that they can buy low later, but their individual actions or behaviors have no substantive effects on financial asset prices; whereas "manipulators" try to do the same thing but their actions, behaviors, and often words, whether under implicit or explicit collusion, have substantial self-fulfilling effects on financial asset prices (e.g., market exchange rates), and they profit handsomely from such transactions in a short time. In this sense, "speculators" are normal and healthy for a functional financial market, while "manipulators" contravene the free and competitive market requirement.

Even if such attacks were launched on those countries perceived to be the weakest, as was actually the case with Thailand in January–June 1997, such an arrangement would have allowed the exchange of information, analyses, and advice, and given a clearer understanding of the nature of the attacks. Such help was clearly needed in the case of Thailand and Malaysia in the early phases of the 1997 crisis. The lack of information on the true positions and alternative defensive strategies of the country under attack would not have been such an issue,[8] for instance, when Thailand requested about $5 billion in short-term liquidity assistance from the PRC and Japan during May–June of that fateful year. The reaction of the two countries might have been different, and the financial crisis that started in Thailand on 2 July 1997 might have been averted or contained. The application of inappropriate conditions under the IMF Program and the contagion toward the rest of East Asia that ensued also might not have occurred.

Second, transparency is a noble concept and essential for the optimal functioning of competitive and complete financial markets. But as rightly pointed out by Joseph Yam, Chief Executive of the Hong Kong Monetary Authority, in his speech to the Wharton School Regional Alumni Meeting in Tokyo on 12 July 2002, transparency must cut both ways with regard to the behavior of both the financial authorities (central banks) and private financial market participants (e.g., hedge funds and banks). The authorities have the responsibility not only to disclose their interventions in financial markets but also to monitor and disclose actions of private participants. Thus, their substantial market influences, if any, can be properly considered and understood by the less influential market participants. Such disclosures must, however, be based on theoretical and empirical analyses of these behaviors and their effects on financial asset prices (exchange rates, stock prices, bond prices, and interest rates), which are different under perfectly

[8] Takatoshi Ito of the University of Tokyo has explained informally the primary reason for Japan's turning down Thailand's request for liquidity assistance in June 1997. It was because the necessary information on the true nature of the forward contract exposures and of the financial conditions of Thailand was not available; the urgency and limited time frame did not allow for a timely affirmative answer. The contagion effects of Thailand's crisis on its neighbors were underestimated and not properly understood.

competitive settings than under oligopolistic micromarket structures. This is the rationale for advocating information monitoring, analysis, exchange, and disclosure among the financial authorities and with the general public, to improve the information content and symmetry of financial markets, to make them more competitive and equitable for all.

Third, with a view toward eventually establishing an Asian Currency Unit and Asian common currency area (ACCA), ASEAN+3 finance ministers and central bank governors must conduct frequent and continuous policy dialogues, peer reviews, and joint decision making on policy coordination in areas of common interests and concerns. These include relationships among short-term portfolio capital movements, exchange rates, stock prices, interest rates, consumer prices, economic growth, international trade, investments, and regional financial cooperation to promote growth and stability, as well as to prevent or manage international financial crises and contagion (see Girardin, this volume).

As a result, all these interrelated issues regarding financial resource pooling and provision; information monitoring, analysis, and swapping; exchange rate regimes and choices; financial market restructuring and development; and intergovernment institutional setups for surveillance and joint decision making must be considered together. Actions must be taken on a joint and coordinated basis as parts of a total system, even though some concrete moves can be taken in a step-by-step manner. Policy dialogue and coordination among the authorities of ASEAN+3 should be an important milestone for developing a new international financial infrastructure for East Asia.

Once all these pieces are put together in a consistent and mutually reinforcing manner through words and actions, centralized resource pooling and provision will emerge naturally. Potential lenders and borrowers will feel comfortable with the perceived sacrifice of national sovereignty and appreciate the usefulness of a regionally based supranational institution for all members. For the sake of clarity and to avoid undue and unnecessary emotional reactions, this regional financial arrangement could be referred to as the Asian Currency Fund (ACF), for its highly focused mandate and operations.

A 15-year action plan for the ASEAN+3 financial authorities

We can now put the preceding analyses together to suggest a set of actions that should be taken bilaterally or multilaterally by all ASEAN+3 countries to create an enhanced CMI and reserve pooling arrangement. At the same time, they would build up the necessary ingredients for eventually achieving a common currency area in East Asia. These actions can be summarized as follows.

(i) Within 1 year from now, the three Northeast Asian countries (PRC, Japan, and Korea) should have completed their one-way BSAs with the 10 ASEAN countries, using the standard agreement (with the 90% IMF program entry clause) already entered into with Thailand and Malaysia. The agreements with Indonesia and the Philippines should be concluded as soon as possible and those for the rest of the ASEAN countries by the end of 2003.

(ii) Thailand should negotiate and conclude two-way BSAs with the PRC and Japan either based on a fully convertible outside currency, as in the case of the existing Korea-Thailand pact, or directly between the two currencies of the signatory countries, as in the case of the existing yuan-yen two-way BSA between the PRC and Japan. The sizes of such two-way BSAs should be negotiated by each pair of countries, and should be in addition to the existing one-way swap agreements. Malaysia, a country that has already signed a one-way swap agreement with Japan, should accelerate the signing of such one-way agreements with the PRC and Korea, perhaps along the lines of those already signed with Thailand. At the same time, Malaysia should also negotiate additional two-way bilateral agreements. Indonesia and the Philippines might, within the next 2 years, also attempt to enter into similar two-way swap agreements with the three Northeast Asian countries.

(iii) It should be noted that the intra-ASEAN swap agreements, which are multilateral in nature, already exist with a total size the equivalent of $10 billion. Leading countries, in terms of international reserves, might want to initiate an increase in the size of this intra-ASEAN facility within the next 2 years.

(iv) Taking the sizes of the swap agreements that are already signed among PRC, Japan, Korea, Malaysia, Philippines, and Thailand, and the (multilateral) 10 ASEAN countries as indicative, it can be estimated that, if all other agreements are signed by June 2004 as suggested in (i) to (iii), the combined size of all agreements should come to about $55 billion–$65 billion (Table 3.5).

(v) Whether or not the combined resources under the currency swap agreements will be adequate depends significantly on the realization of the following set of three envisioned developments in regional financial arrangements. First, foreign exchange regimes among East and Southeast Asian countries may undergo changes from a practically exclusive reliance on the US dollar as a reference currency to an implicit or explicit reliance on a broader set of reference currencies, e.g., the dollar, yen, and euro for most countries. Second, there is likely to be more transparency and focused monitoring over portfolio inflow/outflow activities of private operators in imperfect or thinly traded foreign exchange, stock, bond, and money markets. Third, a process of de-internationalization (if the de facto internationalization was judged to be unintentional or too extreme) or a more gradual regionalization (if internationalization has not taken place) of domestic currencies may be under way.

If these conditions all hold, the post-1997 East Asian region may not need more pooled financial resources to defend their currency values compared with the pre-1997 period. In the earlier period, almost all countries practically pegged their currency values to the US dollar, and there was an unintentional neglect of capital account monitoring and uncontrolled internationalization of many domestic currencies (the Malaysian ringgit, the Thai baht, the Indonesian rupiah, the Philippine peso, and the Korean won).

A less definitive but still affirmative answer can be given even if the PRC and Malaysia continue to peg their currency values 100% to the dollar (hard peg) and other East Asian countries implicitly peg their currency values to baskets of the G-3 countries (soft peg).[9] The $65 billion reserve pool is likely to be adequate to prevent and counteract short-term speculative attacks on currencies, provided that associated actions to be specified in the following sections are also taken in parallel during the next 5–10 years.

(vi) On information gathering, exchange, and analysis, it is suggested that each of the ASEAN+3 countries immediately monitor and make available to others information on short-term portfolio capital inflows and outflows, detailing the types (stocks, bonds, nonresident local currency deposits, bank loans), speeds (how fast they move in and out), and sizes of such movements on a weekly or at least monthly basis. The pool of information can be coordinated and analyzed jointly by all member countries to answer the quantitative question of whether (together with other factors such as interest rate differentials, movements in major currencies, and interventions to stem excessive moves in market exchange rates by monetary authorities) such short-term portfolio capital inflows and outflows have significant influences on the market exchange rates of currencies of the smaller countries in East Asia.

[9] The taxonomy of a free floating exchange rate regime (for major and competitive currency markets such as those of the dollar, yen, and euro) and pegged exchange rate regime (for almost all thinly traded and imperfect currency markets of other East Asian currencies) is preferred. This is as long as the central banks of countries in the latter operate in their domestic foreign exchange markets to buy or sell fully convertible currencies (dollar, yen, euro) and manage their exchange rates and hence international reserve levels in some manner, even though under normal conditions they may not need to intervene daily. The 100% peg to the dollar in the case of the PRC and Malaysia and the current exchange rate regimes of Indonesia, Korea, Philippines, Singapore, and Thailand are more similar to each other than most people may believe. In both cases, the central banks do "manage" their currency values in a "very active" (hard peg) or "rather active" (soft peg) manner through the operations of their exchange equalization funds or similar institutional arrangements. The free floating exchange rate regime, on the other hand, assumes that central banks have no intention or no ability either to intervene or manage their currency values, because the foreign exchange markets of the currencies of these countries are internationalized, large, heavily traded, and perfectly competitive.

Table 3.5 **ASEAN+3 Bilateral Currency Swap Arrangements, as of 19 July 2002** ($ billion)

		Bilateral Swap	
Borrower		**Japan**	**People's Republic of China**
Thailand	Amount	3.0	2.0
	Currency	baht-dollar	baht-dollar
	Nature	one-way	one-way
	Status	concluded (July 2001)	concluded (December 2001)
Malaysia	Amount	3.5	2.0
	Currency	ringgit-dollar	
	Nature	one-way	one-way?
	Status	concluded (October 2001)	under negotiation
Philippines	Amount	3.0	2.0
	Currency	peso-dollar	
	Nature	one-way	one-way?
	Status	concluded (August 2001)	under negotiation
Indonesia	Amount	3.0	2.0
	Currency		
	Nature	one-way?	one-way?
	Status	under negotiation	nil
Viet Nam	Amount	0.0	0.0
	Currency		
	Nature		
	Status		
Lao People's Democratic Republic	Amount	0.0	0.0
	Currency		
	Nature		
	Status		
Cambodia	Amount	0.0	0.0
	Currency		
	Nature		
	Status		
Singapore	Amount	?	0.0
	Currency		
	Nature	one-way?	
	Status	under negotiation	nil
Brunei Darussalam	Amount	0.0	0.0
	Currency		
	Nature		
	Status		
Myanmar	Amount	0.0	0.0
	Currency		
	Nature		
	Status		
Japan	Amount	0.00	3.00
	Currency		yen-yuan
	Nature		two-way
	Status		concluded (March 2002)
People's Republic of China	Amount	3.0	0.0
	Currency	yen-yuan	
	Nature	two-way	
	Status	concluded (March 2002)	
Republic of Korea	Amount	7.0	2.0
	Currency	won-dollar	won-yuan-dollar
	Nature	one-way	two-way
	Status	concluded (July 2001)	concluded (June 2002)
Total		**22.5**	**13.0**

[a] To be expanded to 65 as proposed in the Action Plan. ? means uncertain.
Source: Various.

Arrangements			
Republic of Korea	Subtotal	Intra-ASEAN Swap Arrangements	Total
1.0 two-way concluded (June 2002)	6.0	1.0	7.0
1.0 two-way? under negotiation	6.5	1.0	7.5
1.0 two-way? under negotiation	6.0	1.0	7.0
1.0 two-way? nil	6.0	1.0	7.0
0.0	0.0	1.0	1.0
0.0	0.0	1.0	1.0
0.0	0.0	1.0	1.0
0.0 nil	0.0	1.0	1.0?
0.0	0.0	1.0	1.0
0.0	0.0	1.0	1.0
3.00 yen-won two-way? nil?	6.00	0.00	6.00
2.0 won-yuan-dollar two-way concluded (June 2002)	5.0	0.0	5.0
0.0	9.0	0.0	9.0
9.00	41.5	**10.0**	**54.5[a]?**

Countries that peg their currency values 100% with the US dollar will not be able to perform this empirical analysis, because there is no fluctuation in their currency values relative to the dollar. In such cases, the correlation between short-term portfolio capital inflows or outflows, other things being equal, and the accumulation or depletion of international reserves can still be analyzed. The country exchange equalization funds or currency boards stand ready to buy and sell unlimited amounts of hard currencies to defend the hard peg against the domestic currencies.

(vii) While these developments are taking place, it will be useful if the region's financial authorities exchange ideas about their preferences for currency regimes. This may allow them to coordinate their policies in steps that may eventually lead to something like the European Monetary System (the "Snake") and a common currency area (Ito and Park, this volume).

(viii) Once all BSAs are put in place, the time will be ripe for the ASEAN+3 countries to multilateralize and centralize the reserve pooling process. This can be done, as suggested in the section Resource Pooling and Borrowing Entitlements for ASEAN+3, by agreeing to inject all out-placements of deposits with other monetary authorities in the region that arise from excessive short-term portfolio capital inflows into a central pool called the ACF. This would eventually be administered and managed by a supranational institution with surveillance capabilities and decision-making power on behalf of the financial authorities of the ASEAN+3 countries. Such a centralized pool could be implemented by the end of June 2007. The ACF can be used by member countries for legitimate currency stabilization objectives under a set of clear and specific financial conditions. These conditions will depend on whether imbalances arise due to the volatility of short-term portfolio capital flows or to medium- to long-term fundamental disequilibria in the economies concerned.

This institution will benefit from all the work that has been done in the form of bilateral and multilateral technical studies on enhanced conditionality over and above those of IMF. In a sense, this expanded set of conditions will be stricter than those of IMF. To avoid IMF-style conditionality, each country will have to demonstrate that its short-term international liquidity needs and borrowing requirements are not caused by excessive fiscal deficits, excessive domestic credit expansion, or excessive wage increases. Only if such liquidity replenishment needs are caused by short-term portfolio capital outflows can the borrowing country (a) draw down on its previously accumulated excess reserves, which have earlier been put into the common pool; (b) make use of the deposits it has received from other participating countries; and (c) tap the 90% portion of the currency swap agreements to defend its currency. The borrowing country will repay this short-term loan immediately when short-term capital inflows return.

There may be cases where balance-of-payments instabilities are structural and fundamental in nature, with the large balance-of-payments deficit caused by excessive fiscal deficits, excessive domestic credit expansions, and/or excessive domestic wage increases. It may also be that such incidents coincide with the fact that the liquidity requesting country has never contributed any excess reserves arising from large, short-term, portfolio capital inflows to the common pool. In such cases, the borrowing country must first undertake the traditional IMF policy prescriptions, i.e., tax increases, government expenditure cuts, domestic credit restrictions, nominal wage freezes, etc., before it can make use of the deposits it has received from other central banks or the 90% swap lines to defend the currency peg. In such a case, structural currency realignment will have to precede the use of short-term liquidity assistance from the centralized pool.

(ix) The centralized reserve pooling and provision for justifiable and legitimate purposes must go hand in hand with the establishment of a technically capable surveillance unit within the region. To help build up this surveillance organization, in the short run the ASEAN+3 countries could rely on an EPG backed by a network of technical research institutions (think tanks) from some or all the member countries under the proposed EARFA Forum. The EPG and EARFA forums can bridge the gap until a regional surveillance unit is created and brought up to speed by working together to assist policymakers in taking all the actions that have been recommended within the stipulated timetable. However, the EPG and EARFA forums would eventually be dissolved and parts of them merged by June 2007 into a centralized surveillance organization responsible for administering and managing the ACF, together with its short-term liquidity support and loan repayment collection functions.

After June 2007, issues related to coordination and harmonization of exchange rate regimes among East Asian countries can be studied and debated under a new set of financial conditions and market structures that are more competitive, complete, transparent, and intense. By then, experience in regional surveillance and liquidity provision—and the familiarity and trust that such cooperation will have brought about—will have accumulated to the point where the additional intensification of regional cooperation required to administer a regional exchange rate arrangement may represent a relatively small additional step compared with what it would be today.

Summary and conclusions

The framework for resource provision under the regional financial arrangement as developed and proposed in this study is consistent with a more intense level of cooperation, in the form of a long-term regional exchange rate arrangement for East Asia. In approaching such an ultimate objective strategically, the proposal here is that certain measures must be taken in the meantime, in the form of enhanced regional arrangements for liquidity provision, to prevent the recurrence of new capital account-instigated financial crises. These measures include the following:

First, the ASEAN+3 countries should take steps that would permit existing swap arrangements to be untied from IMF conditionality in the event of capital account crises. To achieve this, each member country's financial authority should develop an effective capital account monitoring system capable of identifying and distinguishing short-term portfolio inflows/outflows from desirable long-term capital flows on a weekly or monthly basis. Restrictions should be imposed on residents' holding of financial assets and liabilities denominated in foreign currencies as well as nonresidents' holding of similar instruments denominated in local currencies. However, this should be accompanied by a step-by-step program to regionalize the domestic currency. In the event that equities and bonds are allowed to be traded across countries, stock markets and securities and exchange commissions must also be brought in to design international settlement/clearing systems for these financial instruments. Under these conditions, the activation of swap lines in the face of crises driven by "hot money" flows can be left to the discretion of lending countries, without a link to IMF-supported programs.

The study has also proposed mechanisms for expanding resources available under regional reserve pooling arrangements. These could preserve the decentralized and multilateral nature of present arrangements by increasing the size of existing swap lines. Or they could take a more centralized form based on a system of cross reserve deposits among member central banks. With this, participating countries are able to draw a multiple of the reserves they have deposited with other central banks, as approved by a regional reserve-management authority, the ACF. The size of the resources needed for availability under either arrangement would depend on the form that future exchange rate coordination takes within the region. Among the two leading contenders for exchange rate coordination—pegging to a single currency and to a basket of the three major currencies—reserve requirements for the former are likely to exceed those for the latter.

Finally, this paper considered the institutional requirements for implementing such enhanced regional arrangements for liquidity provision. In the short run, an EPG, supported by a Technical Forum, could oversee the expanded multilateral and decentralized system of reserve sharing based on swaps. But a move to a more centralized system of resource pooling in the medium term would require creating a regional secretariat to approve the disbursement of funds, establish conditions for their use, and monitor compliance. Cooperation along these lines would lay the basis for coordination of foreign exchange market intervention, possibly leading to common pegs and perhaps to the eventual emergence of an Asian currency unit and a regional currency.

ACKNOWLEDGMENTS

The author is grateful to his colleagues and assistants at the Fiscal Policy Research Institute (FPRI), especially to Dr. Bhasu Bhanich Supapol and Dr. Kanit Sangsubhan. This revised version of the original paper has benefited from discussions with participants of the finalization workshop organized for the ADB Study on Monetary and Financial Cooperation in East Asia at the Asian Development Bank in July 2002.

Table A3.1 **People's Republic of China's (PRC's) Hypothetical Exchange Rate, and Short-Term Reserve Accumulation and Management**

	Average Exchange Rate				PRC's Excess Short-Term Reserves Accumulation ($ million equivalent)			PRC's Operations ($ million)			
									Central Bank's Intervention		
Period	Yen/$	Euro/$	Yuan/$	Average SSE Index	Central Bank's Purchase (+) from Short-Term Capital Inflows	Managed by Own Central Bank (60%)	Placed with Other Central Banks (40%)	Central Bank's Purchase (+) from Short-Term Capital Inflows	Using Excess Short-Term Reserves Placed at Own Central Bank (60%)	Using Excess Short-Term Reserves Placed with Other Central Banks (40%)	Using Bilateral Swap Agreements
Jan 02	132.94	1.1578	8	420	100	60	40	100	0	0	0
Feb 02	133.89	1.1559	8	434	200	120	80	200	0	0	0
Mar 02	132.71	1.1463	8	467	300	180	120	300	0	0	0
Apr 02	127.97	1.1101	8	485	350	210	140	350	0	0	0
May 02	123.96	1.0929	8	448	50	30	20	50	0	0	0
Jun 02	122.00	1.0756	8	468	150	90	60	150	0	0	0
Jul 02	120.00	1.0580	8	488	150	90	60	150	0	0	0
Aug 02	118.00	1.0403	8	508	150	90	60	150	0	0	0
Sep 02	116.00	1.0227	8	528	150	90	60	150	0	0	0
Oct 02	114.00	1.0051	8	548	150	90	60	150	0	0	0
Nov 02	112.00	0.9874	8	568	150	90	60	150	0	0	0
Dec 02	110.00	0.9698	8	588	150	90	60	150	0	0	0
Jan 03	111.00	0.9786	8	573	-100	0	0	-100	100	0	0
Feb 03	112.00	0.9874	8	558	-100	0	0	-100	100	0	0
Mar 03	113.00	0.9962	8	543	-100	0	0	-100	100	0	0
Apr 03	114.00	1.0051	8	528	-100	0	0	-100	100	0	0
May 03	115.00	1.0139	8	513	-100	0	0	-100	100	0	0
Jun 03	116.00	1.0227	8	498	-100	0	0	-100	100	0	0
Jul 03	117.00	1.0315	8	483	-100	0	0	-100	100	0	0
Aug 03	118.00	1.0403	8	468	-100	0	0	-100	100	0	0
Sep 03	119.00	1.0491	8	453	-100	0	0	-100	100	0	0
Oct 03	120.00	1.0580	8	438	-100	0	0	-100	100	0	0
Nov 03	121.00	1.0668	8	423	-100	0	0	-100	100	0	0
Dec 03	122.00	1.0756	8	408	-100	0	0	-100	100	0	0

SSE = Shanghai Stock Exchange.

Table A3.2 **People's Bank of China Out-Placements with Other Central Banks as a Result of Excessive Short-Term Capital Inflows Absorbed by the Central Bank** ($ million)

Period	Japan	Republic of Korea	Singapore	Thailand	Malaysia	Indonesia	Philippines	Total for People's Republic of China
Jan 02	23.51	6.01	4.43	1.93	1.80	1.64	0.67	40.00
Feb 02	47.02	12.03	8.87	3.86	3.61	3.28	1.33	80.00
Mar 02	70.54	18.04	13.30	5.79	5.41	4.92	2.00	120.00
Apr 02	82.29	21.05	15.52	6.75	6.32	5.74	2.33	140.00
May 02	11.76	3.01	2.22	0.96	0.90	0.82	0.33	20.00
Jun 02	35.27	9.02	6.65	2.89	2.71	2.46	1.00	60.00
Jul 02	35.27	9.02	6.65	2.89	2.71	2.46	1.00	60.00
Aug 02	35.27	9.02	6.65	2.89	2.71	2.46	1.00	60.00
Sep 02	35.27	9.02	6.65	2.89	2.71	2.46	1.00	60.00
Oct 02	35.27	9.02	6.65	2.89	2.71	2.46	1.00	60.00
Nov 02	35.27	9.02	6.65	2.89	2.71	2.46	1.00	60.00
Dec 02	35.27	9.02	6.65	2.89	2.71	2.46	1.00	60.00
Total out-placement by country	482.00	123.30	90.89	39.56	36.99	33.59	13.66	820.00

Note: Assuming that all agreements as proposed in this study were in place from Jan 02 and People's Republic of China's currency swap agreements with Japan and Republic of Korea are modified to have this study's conditionality, not the International Monetary Fund's.

Table A3.3 **International Reserve by Country and Proportion at End-December 2001, to Be Used by People's Bank of China for Deposit Out-Placements**

Item	Japan	Republic of Korea	Singapore	Thailand	Malaysia	Indonesia	Philippines	Total for People's Republic of China
International reserve ($ million)	401,959	102,821	75,800	32,993	30,848	28,016	11,391	683,828
Proportion	0.59	0.15	0.11	0.05	0.05	0.04	0.02	1.00

Table A3.4 **Indonesia's Hypothetical Exchange Rate, and Short-Term Reserve Accumulation and Management**

	Average Exchange Rate				Indonesia's Excess Short-Term Reserves Accumulation ($ million equivalent)			Indonesia's Operations ($ million)			
									Central Bank's Intervention		
Period	Yen/$	Euro/$	Rupiah/$	Jakarta Stock Exchange Index	Central Bank's $ Purchase (+) from Short-Term Capital Inflows	Managed by Own Central Bank (60%)	Placed with Other Central Banks (40%)	Central Bank's Purchase (+) from Short-Term Capital Inflows	Using Excess Short-Term Reserves Placed at Own Central Bank (60%)	Using Excess Short-Term Reserves Placed with Other Central Banks (40%)	Using Bilateral Swap Agreements
Jan 02	132.94	1.1578	10320	451.64	60	36	24	60	0	0	0
Feb 02	133.89	1.1559	10189	453.25	50	30	20	50	0	0	0
Mar 02	132.71	1.1463	9655	481.78	80	48	32	80	0	0	0
Apr 02	127.97	1.1101	9316	534.06	120	72	48	120	0	0	0
May 02	123.96	1.0929	8785	530.79	100	60	40	100	0	0	0
Jun 02	122.00	1.0756	8722	560.79	100	60	40	100	0	0	0
Jul 02	120.00	1.0580	8659	590.79	100	60	40	100	0	0	0
Aug 02	118.00	1.0403	8595	620.79	100	60	40	100	0	0	0
Sep 02	116.00	1.0227	8531	650.79	100	60	40	100	0	0	0
Oct 02	114.00	1.0051	8467	680.79	100	60	40	100	0	0	0
Nov 02	112.00	0.9874	8404	710.79	100	60	40	100	0	0	0
Dec 02	110.00	0.9698	8340	740.79	100	60	40	100	0	0	0
Jan 03	111.00	0.9786	8371	710.79	-150	0	0	-150	150	0	0
Feb 03	112.00	0.9874	8403	680.79	-150	0	0	-150	150	0	0
Mar 03	113.00	0.9962	8435	650.79	-150	0	0	-150	150	0	0
Apr 03	114.00	1.0051	8467	620.79	-150	0	0	-150	150	0	0
May 03	115.00	1.0139	8499	590.79	-150	0	0	-150	66	86	0
Jun 03	116.00	1.0227	8531	560.79	-150	0	0	-150	0	150	0
Jul 03	117.00	1.0315	8563	530.79	-150	0	0	-150	0	150	0
Aug 03	118.00	1.0403	8594	500.79	-150	0	0	-150	0	144	6
Sep 03	119.00	1.0491	8626	470.79	-150	0	0	-150	0	0	150
Oct 03	120.00	1.0580	8658	440.79	-150	0	0	-150	0	0	150
Nov 03	121.00	1.0668	8690	410.79	-150	0	0	-150	0	0	150
Dec 03	122.00	1.0756	8722	380.79	-150	0	0	-150	0	0	150

Note: Data from Jan 02 to May 02 are actual, those for Jun 02 and after are estimates only.

Table A3.5 **Bank of Indonesia Out-Placements with Other Central Banks as a Result of Excessive Short-Term Capital Inflows Absorbed by the Central Bank** ($ million)

Period	Japan	People's Republic of China	Republic of Korea	Singapore	Thailand	Malaysia	Philippines	Total for Indonesia
Jan 02	11.11	5.87	2.84	2.10	0.91	0.85	0.31	24.00
Feb 02	9.26	4.89	2.37	1.75	0.76	0.71	0.26	20.00
Mar 02	14.82	7.82	3.79	2.79	1.22	1.14	0.42	32.00
Apr 02	22.23	11.73	5.69	4.19	1.82	1.71	0.63	48.00
May 02	18.52	9.78	4.74	3.49	1.52	1.42	0.52	40.00
Jun 02	18.52	9.78	4.74	3.49	1.52	1.42	0.52	40.00
Jul 02	18.52	9.78	4.74	3.49	1.52	1.42	0.52	40.00
Aug 02	18.52	9.78	4.74	3.49	1.52	1.42	0.52	40.00
Sep 02	18.52	9.78	4.74	3.49	1.52	1.42	0.52	40.00
Oct 02	18.52	9.78	4.74	3.49	1.52	1.42	0.52	40.00
Nov 02	18.52	9.78	4.74	3.49	1.52	1.42	0.52	40.00
Dec 02	18.52	9.78	4.74	3.49	1.52	1.42	0.52	40.00
Total out-placement by country	205.62	108.53	52.60	38.77	16.88	15.78	5.83	444.00

Note: Assuming that all agreements as proposed in this study were in place from Jan 02 and Indonesia's currency swap agreements with Japan, People's Republic of China, and Republic of Korea are modified to have this study's conditionality, not the International Monetary Fund's.

Table A3.6 **Japan's Hypothetical Exchange Rate, and Short-Term Reserve Accumulation and Management**

					Japan's Excess Short-Term Reserves Accumulation ($ million equivalent)			Japan's Operations ($ million)			
	Average Exchange Rate								Central Bank's Intervention		
Period	Yen/$	Euro/$	Yen/$	Average NIKKEI Index	Central Bank's Purchase (+) from Short-Term Capital Inflows	Managed by Own Central Bank (60%)	Placed with Other Central Banks (40%)	Central Bank's Purchase (+) from Short-Term Capital Inflows	Using Excess Short-Term Reserves Placed at Own Central Bank (60%)	Using Excess Short-Term Reserves Placed with Other Central Banks (40%)	Using Bilateral Swap Agreements
Jan 02	132.94	1.1578	133	9998	100	60	40	100	0	0	0
Feb 02	133.89	1.1559	134	10588	200	120	80	200	0	0	0
Mar 02	132.71	1.1463	131	11025	100	60	40	100	0	0	0
Apr 02	127.97	1.1101	131	11493	300	180	120	300	0	0	0
May 02	123.96	1.0929	127	11764	300	180	120	300	0	0	0
Jun 02	122.00	1.0756	122	11964	150	90	60	150	0	0	0
Jul 02	120.00	1.0580	120	12164	150	90	60	150	0	0	0
Aug 02	118.00	1.0403	118	12364	150	90	60	150	0	0	0
Sep 02	116.00	1.0227	116	12564	150	90	60	150	0	0	0
Oct 02	114.00	1.0051	114	12764	150	90	60	150	0	0	0
Nov 02	112.00	0.9874	112	12964	150	90	60	150	0	0	0
Dec 02	110.00	0.9698	110	13164	150	90	60	150	0	0	0
Jan 03	111.00	0.9786	111	12964	-150	0	0	-150	150	0	0
Feb 03	112.00	0.9874	112	12764	-150	0	0	-150	150	0	0
Mar 03	113.00	0.9962	113	12564	-150	0	0	-150	150	0	0
Apr 03	114.00	1.0051	114	12364	-150	0	0	-150	150	0	0
May 03	115.00	1.0139	115	12164	-150	0	0	-150	150	0	0
Jun 03	116.00	1.0227	116	11964	-150	0	0	-150	150	0	0
Jul 03	117.00	1.0315	117	11764	-150	0	0	-150	150	0	0
Aug 03	118.00	1.0403	118	11564	-150	0	0	-150	150	0	0
Sep 03	119.00	1.0491	119	11364	-150	0	0	-150	30	120	0
Oct 03	120.00	1.0580	120	11164	-150	0	0	-150	0	150	0
Nov 03	121.00	1.0668	121	10964	-150	0	0	-150	0	150	0
Dec 03	122.00	1.0756	122	10764	-150	0	0	-150	0	150	0

NIKKEI = Nikkei Stock Price.
Note: Data from Jan 02 to May 02 are actual, those for Jun 02 and after are estimates only.

Table A3.7 **Bank of Japan Out-Placements with Other Central Banks as a Result of Excessive Short-Term Capital Inflows Absorbed by the Central Bank** ($ million)

Period	People's Republic of China	Republic of Korea	Singapore	Thailand	Malaysia	Indonesia	Philippines	Total for Japan
Jan 02	50.68	26.75	9.56	4.16	3.89	3.53	1.44	100.00
Feb 02	60.81	32.10	11.47	4.99	4.67	4.24	1.72	120.00
Mar 02	70.95	37.45	13.38	5.82	5.44	4.94	2.01	140.00
Apr 02	20.27	10.70	3.82	1.66	1.56	1.41	0.57	40.00
May 02	10.14	5.35	1.91	0.83	0.78	0.71	0.29	20.00
Jun 02	20.27	10.70	3.82	1.66	1.56	1.41	0.57	40.00
Jul 02	20.27	10.70	3.82	1.66	1.56	1.41	0.57	40.00
Aug 02	20.27	10.70	3.82	1.66	1.56	1.41	0.57	40.00
Sep 02	20.27	10.70	3.82	1.66	1.56	1.41	0.57	40.00
Oct 02	20.27	10.70	3.82	1.66	1.56	1.41	0.57	40.00
Nov 02	20.27	10.70	3.82	1.66	1.56	1.41	0.57	40.00
Dec 02	20.27	10.70	3.82	1.66	1.56	1.41	0.57	40.00
Total out-placement by country	354.74	187.24	66.90	29.12	27.22	24.72	10.05	700.00

Note: Assuming that all agreements as proposed in this study were in place from Jan 02 and Japan's currency swap agreements with People's Republic of China and Republic of Korea are modified to have this study's conditionality, not the International Monetary Fund's.

Table A3.8 **International Reserve by Country and Proportion at End-December 2001, to Be Used by Bank of Japan for Deposit Out-Placements**

Item	People's Republic of China	Republic of Korea	Singapore	Thailand	Malaysia	Indonesia	Philippines	Total for Japan
International reserve ($ million)	212,165	102,821	75,800	32,993	30,848	28,016	11,391	494,034
Proportion	0.43	0.21	0.15	0.07	0.06	0.06	0.02	1.00

Table A3.9 **Malaysia's Hypothetical Exchange Rate, and Short-Term Reserve Accumulation and Management**

Period	Average Exchange Rate			KLSE Index	Malaysia's Excess Short-Term Reserves Accumulation ($ million equivalent)			Malaysia's Operations ($ million)			
									Central Bank's Intervention		
	Yen/$	Euro/$	Ringgit/$		Central Bank's Purchase (+) from Short-Term Capital Inflows	Managed by Own Central Bank (60%)	Placed with Other Central Banks (40%)	Central Bank's Purchase (+) from Short-Term Capital Inflows	Using Excess Short-Term Reserves Placed at Own Central Bank (60%)	Using Excess Short-Term Reserves Placed with Other Central Banks (40%)	Using Bilateral Swap Agreements
Jan 02	132.94	1.1578	3.80	718.82	200	120	80	200	0	0	0
Feb 02	133.89	1.1559	3.80	708.91	150	90	60	150	0	0	0
Mar 02	132.71	1.1463	3.80	756.10	250	150	100	250	0	0	0
Apr 02	127.97	1.1101	3.80	793.99	275	165	110	275	0	0	0
May 02	123.96	1.0929	3.80	741.76	100	60	40	100	0	0	0
Jun 02	122.00	1.0756	3.77	766.76	100	60	40	100	0	0	0
Jul 02	120.00	1.0580	3.75	791.76	100	60	40	100	0	0	0
Aug 02	118.00	1.0403	3.72	816.76	100	60	40	100	0	0	0
Sep 02	116.00	1.0227	3.69	841.76	100	60	40	100	0	0	0
Oct 02	114.00	1.0051	3.66	866.76	100	60	40	100	0	0	0
Nov 02	112.00	0.9874	3.64	891.76	100	60	40	100	0	0	0
Dec 02	110.00	0.9698	3.61	916.76	100	60	40	100	0	0	0
Jan 03	111.00	0.9786	3.62	896.76	-80	0	0	-80	80	0	0
Feb 03	112.00	0.9874	3.64	876.76	-80	0	0	-80	80	0	0
Mar 03	113.00	0.9962	3.65	856.76	-80	0	0	-80	80	0	0
Apr 03	114.00	1.0051	3.66	836.76	-80	0	0	-80	80	0	0
May 03	115.00	1.0139	3.68	816.76	-80	0	0	-80	80	0	0
Jun 03	116.00	1.0227	3.69	796.76	-80	0	0	-80	80	0	0
Jul 03	117.00	1.0315	3.70	776.76	-80	0	0	-80	80	0	0
Aug 03	118.00	1.0403	3.72	756.76	-80	0	0	-80	80	0	0
Sep 03	119.00	1.0491	3.73	736.76	-80	0	0	-80	80	0	0
Oct 03	120.00	1.0580	3.75	716.76	-80	0	0	-80	80	0	0
Nov 03	121.00	1.0668	3.76	696.76	-80	0	0	-80	80	0	0
Dec 03	122.00	1.0756	3.77	676.76	-80	0	0	-80	80	0	0

KLSE = Kuala Lumpur Stock Exchange.
Note: Data from Jan 02 to May 02 are actual, those for Jun 02 and after are estimates only.

Table A3.10 **Bank Negara Malaysia Out-Placements with Other Central Banks as a Result of Excessive Short-Term Capital Inflows Absorbed by the Central Bank** ($ million)

Period	Japan	People's Republic of China	Republic of Korea	Singapore	Thailand	Indonesia	Philippines	Total for Malaysia
Jan 02	37.17	19.62	9.51	7.01	3.05	2.59	1.05	80.00
Feb 02	27.88	14.71	7.13	5.26	2.29	1.94	0.79	60.00
Mar 02	46.46	24.52	11.88	8.76	3.81	3.24	1.32	100.00
Apr 02	51.11	26.98	13.07	9.64	4.19	3.56	1.45	110.00
May 02	18.58	9.81	4.75	3.50	1.53	1.30	0.53	40.00
Jun 02	18.58	9.81	4.75	3.50	1.53	1.30	0.53	40.00
Jul 02	18.58	9.81	4.75	3.50	1.53	1.30	0.53	40.00
Aug 02	18.58	9.81	4.75	3.50	1.53	1.30	0.53	40.00
Sep 02	18.58	9.81	4.75	3.50	1.53	1.30	0.53	40.00
Oct 02	18.58	9.81	4.75	3.50	1.53	1.30	0.53	40.00
Nov 02	18.58	9.81	4.75	3.50	1.53	1.30	0.53	40.00
Dec 02	18.58	9.81	4.75	3.50	1.53	1.30	0.53	40.00
Total out-placement by country	311.29	164.31	79.63	58.70	25.55	21.70	8.82	670.00

Note: Assuming that all agreements as proposed in this study were in place from Jan 02.

Table A3.11 **International Reserve by Country and Proportion at End-December 2001, to Be Used by Bank Negara Malaysia for Deposit Out-Placements**

Item	Japan	People's Republic of China	Republic of Korea	Singapore	Thailand	Indonesia	Philippines	Total for Malaysia
International reserve ($ million)	401,959	212,165	102,821	75,800	32,993	28,016	11,391	865,145
Proportion	0.46	0.25	0.12	0.09	0.04	0.03	0.01	1.00

Table A3.12 **Philippines' Hypothetical Exchange Rate, and Short-Term Reserve Accumulation and Management**

					Philippines' Excess Short-Term Reserves Accumulation ($ million equivalent)			Philippines' Operations ($ million)			
	Average Exchange Rate								Central Bank's Intervention		
Period	Yen/$	Euro/$	Peso/$	PSE Index	Central Bank's Purchase (+) from Short-Term Capital Inflows	Managed by Own Central Bank (60%)	Placed with Other Central Banks (40%)	Central Bank's Purchase (+) from Short-Term Capital Inflows	Using Excess Short-Term Reserves Placed at Own Central Bank (60%)	Using Excess Short-Term Reserves Placed with Other Central Banks (40%)	Using Bilateral Swap Agreements
Jan 02	132.94	1.1578	51	1361.94	20	12	8	20	0	0	0
Feb 02	133.89	1.1559	51	1406.22	10	6	4	10	0	0	0
Mar 02	132.71	1.1463	51	1403.62	30	18	12	30	0	0	0
Apr 02	127.97	1.1101	51	1346.09	20	12	8	20	0	0	0
May 02	123.96	1.0929	50	1315.00	10	6	4	10	0	0	0
Jun 02	122.00	1.0756	50	1345.00	50	30	20	50	0	0	0
Jul 02	120.00	1.0580	50	1375.00	50	30	20	50	0	0	0
Aug 02	118.00	1.0403	49	1405.00	50	30	20	50	0	0	0
Sep 02	116.00	1.0227	49	1435.00	50	30	20	50	0	0	0
Oct 02	114.00	1.0051	48	1465.00	50	30	20	50	0	0	0
Nov 02	112.00	0.9874	48	1495.00	50	30	20	50	0	0	0
Dec 02	110.00	0.9698	48	1525.00	50	30	20	50	0	0	0
Jan 03	111.00	0.9786	47.89	1495.00	-50	0	0	-50	50	0	0
Feb 03	112.00	0.9874	48.07	1465.00	-50	0	0	-50	50	0	0
Mar 03	113.00	0.9962	48.25	1435.00	-50	0	0	-50	50	0	0
Apr 03	114.00	1.0051	48.43	1405.00	-50	0	0	-50	50	0	0
May 03	115.00	1.0139	48.62	1375.00	-50	0	0	-50	50	0	0
Jun 03	116.00	1.0227	48.80	1345.00	-50	0	0	-50	14	36	0
Jul 03	117.00	1.0315	48.98	1315.00	-50	0	0	-50	0	50	0
Aug 03	118.00	1.0403	49.16	1285.00	-50	0	0	-50	0	50	0
Sep 03	119.00	1.0491	49.35	1255.00	-50	0	0	-50	0	40	10
Oct 03	120.00	1.0580	49.53	1225.00	-50	0	0	-50	0	0	50
Nov 03	121.00	1.0668	49.71	1195.00	-50	0	0	-50	0	0	50
Dec 03	122.00	1.0756	49.89	1165.00	-50	0	0	-50	0	0	50

PSE = Philippine Stock Exchange.
Note: Data from Jan 02 to May 02 are actual, those for Jun 02 and after are estimates only.

Table A3.13 **Bangko Sentral ng Pilipinas Out-Placements with Other Central Banks as a Result of Excessive Short-Term Capital Inflows Absorbed by the Central Bank** ($ million)

Period	Japan	People's Republic of China	Republic of Korea	Singapore	Thailand	Malaysia	Indonesia	Total for Philippines
Jan 02	3.70	1.96	0.95	0.70	0.30	0.28	0.10	8.00
Feb 02	1.85	0.98	0.47	0.35	0.15	0.14	0.05	4.00
Mar 02	5.56	2.93	1.42	1.05	0.46	0.43	0.16	12.00
Apr 02	3.70	1.96	0.95	0.70	0.30	0.28	0.10	8.00
May 02	1.85	0.98	0.47	0.35	0.15	0.14	0.05	4.00
Jun 02	9.26	4.89	2.37	1.75	0.76	0.71	0.26	20.00
Jul 02	9.26	4.89	2.37	1.75	0.76	0.71	0.26	20.00
Aug 02	9.26	4.89	2.37	1.75	0.76	0.71	0.26	20.00
Sep 02	9.26	4.89	2.37	1.75	0.76	0.71	0.26	20.00
Oct 02	9.26	4.89	2.37	1.75	0.76	0.71	0.26	20.00
Nov 02	9.26	4.89	2.37	1.75	0.76	0.71	0.26	20.00
Dec 02	9.26	4.89	2.37	1.75	0.76	0.71	0.26	20.00
Total out-placement by country	81.51	43.02	20.85	6.69	15.37	6.26	2.31	176.00

Note: Assuming that all agreements as proposed in this study were in place from Jan 02 and Philippines' currency swap agreements with Japan, People's Republic of China, and Republic of Korea are modified to have this study's conditionality, not the International Monetary Fund's.

Table A3.14 **International Reserve by Country and Proportion at End-December 2001, to Be Used by Bangko Sentral ng Pilipinas for Deposit Out-Placements**

Item	Japan	People's Republic of China	Republic of Korea	Singapore	Thailand	Malaysia	Indonesia	Total for Philippines
International reserve ($ million)	401,959	212,165	102,821	75,800	32,993	30,848	28,016	884,603
Proportion	0.45	0.24	0.12	0.09	0.04	0.03	0.03	1.00

Table A3.15 **Singapore's Hypothetical Exchange Rate, and Short-Term Reserve Accumulation and Management**

Period	Average Exchange Rate			Average SES Index	Singapore's Excess Short-Term Reserves Accumulation ($ million equivalent)			Singapore's Operations ($ million)			
									Monetary Authority's Intervention		
	Yen/$	Euro/$	S$/$		Monetary Authority's Purchase (+) from Short-Term Capital Inflows	Managed by Own Monetary Authority (60%)	Placed with Other Central Banks (40%)	Monetary Authority's Purchase (+) from Short-Term Capital Inflows	Using Excess Short-Term Reserves Placed at Own Central Bank (60%)	Using Excess Short-Term Reserves Placed with Other Central Banks (40%)	Using Bilateral Swap Agreements
Jan 02	132.94	1.1578	1.84	1786.89	300	180	120	300	0	0	0
Feb 02	133.89	1.1559	1.83	1715.58	200	120	80	200	0	0	0
Mar 02	132.71	1.1463	1.83	1803.22	150	90	60	150	0	0	0
Apr 02	127.97	1.1101	1.83	1725.37	50	30	20	50	0	0	0
May 02	123.96	1.0929	1.80	1671.84	25	15	10	25	0	0	0
Jun 02	122.00	1.0756	1.79	1731.84	200	120	80	200	0	0	0
Jul 02	120.00	1.0580	1.78	1791.84	200	120	80	200	0	0	0
Aug 02	118.00	1.0403	1.76	1851.84	200	120	80	200	0	0	0
Sep 02	116.00	1.0227	1.75	1911.84	200	120	80	200	0	0	0
Oct 02	114.00	1.0051	1.74	1971.84	200	120	80	200	0	0	0
Nov 02	112.00	0.9874	1.72	2031.84	200	120	80	200	0	0	0
Dec 02	110.00	0.9698	1.71	2091.84	200	120	80	200	0	0	0
Jan 03	111.00	0.9786	1.72	2031.84	-150	0	0	-150	150	0	0
Feb 03	112.00	0.9874	1.72	1991.84	-150	0	0	-150	150	0	0
Mar 03	113.00	0.9962	1.73	1951.84	-150	0	0	-150	150	0	0
Apr 03	114.00	1.0051	1.74	1911.84	-150	0	0	-150	150	0	0
May 03	115.00	1.0139	1.74	1871.84	-150	0	0	-150	150	0	0
Jun 03	116.00	1.0227	1.75	1831.84	-150	0	0	-150	150	0	0
Jul 03	117.00	1.0315	1.76	1791.84	-150	0	0	-150	150	0	0
Aug 03	118.00	1.0403	1.76	1751.84	-150	0	0	-150	150	0	0
Sep 03	119.00	1.0491	1.77	1711.84	-150	0	0	-150	75	75	0
Oct 03	120.00	1.0580	1.78	1671.84	-150	0	0	-150	0	150	0
Nov 03	121.00	1.0668	1.78	1631.84	-150	0	0	-150	0	150	0
Dec 03	122.00	1.0756	1.79	1591.84	-150	0	0	-150	0	150	0

SES = Singapore Stock Exchange.

Table A3.16 **Bank of Singapore Out-Placements with Other Central Banks as a Result of Excessive Short-Term Capital Inflows Absorbed by the Central Bank** ($ million)

Period	Japan	People's Republic of China	Republic of Korea	Thailand	Malaysia	Indonesia	Philippines	Total for Singapore
Jan 02	58.81	31.04	15.04	4.83	4.51	4.10	1.67	120.00
Feb 02	39.21	20.69	10.03	3.22	3.01	2.73	1.11	80.00
Mar 02	29.40	15.52	7.52	2.41	2.26	2.05	0.83	60.00
Apr 02	9.80	5.17	2.51	0.80	0.75	0.68	0.28	20.00
May 02	4.90	2.59	1.25	0.40	0.38	0.34	0.14	10.00
Jun 02	39.21	20.69	10.03	3.22	3.01	2.73	1.11	80.00
Jul 02	39.21	20.69	10.03	3.22	3.01	2.73	1.11	80.00
Aug 02	39.21	20.69	10.03	3.22	3.01	2.73	1.11	80.00
Sep 02	39.21	20.69	10.03	3.22	3.01	2.73	1.11	80.00
Oct 02	39.21	20.69	10.03	3.22	3.01	2.73	1.11	80.00
Nov 02	39.21	20.69	10.03	3.22	3.01	2.73	1.11	80.00
Dec 02	39.21	20.69	10.03	3.22	3.01	2.73	1.11	80.00
Total out-placement by country	416.57	219.88	106.56	34.19	31.97	29.03	11.80	850.00

Note: Assuming that all agreements as proposed in this study were in place from Jan 02 and Singapore's currency swap agreements with Japan, People's Republic of China, and Republic of Korea are modified to have this study's conditionality, not the International Monetary Fund's.

Table A3.17 **International Reserve by Country and Proportion at End-December 2001, to Be Used by Monetary Authority of Singapore for Deposit Out-Placements**

Item	Japan	People's Republic of China	Republic of Korea	Thailand	Malaysia	Indonesia	Philippines	Total for Singapore
International reserve ($ million)	401,959	212,165	102,821	32,993	30,848	28,016	11,391	820,193
Proportion	0.49	0.26	0.13	0.04	0.04	0.03	0.01	1.00

Table A3.18 **Republic of Korea's Hypothetical Exchange Rate, and Short-Term Reserve Accumulation and Management**

	Average Exchange Rate				Korea's Excess Short-Term Reserves Accumulation ($ million equivalent)			Korea's Operations ($ million)			
									Central Bank's Intervention		
Period	Yen/$	Euro/$	Won/$	Average KOSPI Index	Central Bank's Purchase (+) from Short-Term Capital Inflows	Managed by Own Central Bank (60%)	Placed with Other Central Banks (40%)	Central Bank's Purchase (+) from Short-Term Capital Inflows	Using Excess Short-Term Reserves Placed at Own Central Bank (60%)	Using Excess Short-Term Reserves Placed with Other Central Banks (40%)	Using Bilateral Swap Agreements
Jan 02	132.94	1.1578	1318	92.99	250	150	100	250	0	0	0
Feb 02	133.89	1.1559	1319	102.62	300	180	120	300	0	0	0
Mar 02	132.71	1.1463	1323	111.84	350	210	140	350	0	0	0
Apr 02	127.97	1.1101	1319	106.39	100	60	40	100	0	0	0
May 02	123.96	1.0929	1266	100.80	50	30	20	50	0	0	0
Jun 02	122.00	1.0756	1257	110.80	100	60	40	100	0	0	0
Jul 02	120.00	1.0580	1248	120.80	100	60	40	100	0	0	0
Aug 02	118.00	1.0403	1239	130.80	100	60	40	100	0	0	0
Sep 02	116.00	1.0227	1230	140.80	100	60	40	100	0	0	0
Oct 02	114.00	1.0051	1221	150.80	100	60	40	100	0	0	0
Nov 02	112.00	0.9874	1211	160.80	100	60	40	100	0	0	0
Dec 02	110.00	0.9698	1202	170.80	100	60	40	100	0	0	0
Jan 03	111.00	0.9786	1207	165.80	-50	0	0	-50	50	0	0
Feb 03	112.00	0.9874	1211	160.80	-50	0	0	-50	50	0	0
Mar 03	113.00	0.9962	1216	155.80	-50	0	0	-50	50	0	0
Apr 03	114.00	1.0051	1221	150.80	-50	0	0	-50	50	0	0
May 03	115.00	1.0139	1225	145.80	-50	0	0	-50	50	0	0
Jun 03	116.00	1.0227	1230	140.80	-50	0	0	-50	50	0	0
Jul 03	117.00	1.0315	1234	135.80	-50	0	0	-50	50	0	0
Aug 03	118.00	1.0403	1239	130.80	-50	0	0	-50	50	0	0
Sep 03	119.00	1.0491	1244	125.80	-50	0	0	-50	50	0	0
Oct 03	120.00	1.0580	1248	120.80	-50	0	0	-50	50	0	0
Nov 03	121.00	1.0668	1253	115.80	-50	0	0	-50	50	0	0
Dec 03	122.00	1.0756	1257	110.80	-50	0	0	-50	50	0	0

KOSPI = Korean Stock Price.

Note: Data from Jan 02 to May 02 are actual, those for Jun 02 and after are estimates only.

Table A3.19 **Bank of Korea Out-Placements with Other Central Banks as a Result of Excessive Short-Term Capital Inflows Absorbed by the Central Bank** ($ million)

Period	Japan	People's Republic of China	Singapore	Thailand	Malaysia	Indonesia	Philippines	Total for Republic of Korea
Jan 02	50.68	26.75	9.56	4.16	3.89	3.53	1.44	100.00
Feb 02	60.81	32.10	11.47	4.99	4.67	4.24	1.72	120.00
Mar 02	70.95	37.45	13.38	5.82	5.44	4.94	2.01	140.00
Apr 02	20.27	10.70	3.82	1.66	1.56	1.41	0.57	40.00
May 02	10.14	5.35	1.91	0.83	0.78	0.71	0.29	20.00
Jun 02	20.27	10.70	3.82	1.66	1.56	1.41	0.57	40.00
Jul 02	20.27	10.70	3.82	1.66	1.56	1.41	0.57	40.00
Aug 02	20.27	10.70	3.82	1.66	1.56	1.41	0.57	40.00
Sep 02	20.27	10.70	3.82	1.66	1.56	1.41	0.57	40.00
Oct 02	20.27	10.70	3.82	1.66	1.56	1.41	0.57	40.00
Nov 02	20.27	10.70	3.82	1.66	1.56	1.41	0.57	40.00
Dec 02	20.27	10.70	3.82	1.66	1.56	1.41	0.57	40.00
Total out-placement by country	354.74	187.24	66.90	29.12	27.22	24.72	10.05	700.00

Note: Assuming that all arrangements as proposed in this study were in place from Jan 02 and the Republic of Korea's currency swap agreements with Japan and the People's Republic of China are modified to have this study's conditionality, not the International Monetary Fund's.

Table A3.20 **International Reserve by Country and Proportion at End-December 2001, to Be Used by Bank of Korea for Deposit Out-Placements**

Item	Japan	People's Republic of China	Singapore	Thailand	Malaysia	Indonesia	Philippines	Total for Republic of Korea
International reserve ($ million)	401,959	212,165	75,800	32,993	30,848	28,016	11,391	793,172
Proportion	0.51	0.27	0.10	0.04	0.04	0.04	0.01	1.00

4 Exchange rate regimes in East Asia

TAKATOSHI ITO AND YUNG CHUL PARK

This core study considers the possible exchange rate regimes for East Asia[1] for the immediate future as well as the longer term, as presented in seven background papers (volume 2). The recommendations of those studies cover the entire spectrum of possible exchange rate regimes, ranging from the country-by-country adoption of floating exchange rates to region-wide dollarization. These diverse recommendations are not indicative of a state of confusion regarding appropriate exchange rate regimes for the region. Rather, they provide a possible road map starting where the region is now—a mix of uncoordinated exchange rate regimes—to an eventual (20–30 years later) currency union in the region.

The study has four major sections. The first is a general discussion of the issues involved in the choice of optimal exchange rate regimes. The second gives the pros and cons of specific regimes. The third analyzes how exchange rate arrangements are likely to evolve in the future, given other possible developments in the region. The last section sets out a road map to guide the region

[1] In this core study, East Asia refers to the ASEAN-5 countries (Indonesia, Malaysia, Philippines, Singapore, and Thailand) as well as the People's Republic of China; Hong Kong, China; Japan; Republic of Korea; and Taipei,China.

from the present uncoordinated exchange rate arrangements to possible monetary union.

Exchange rate regimes

The spectrum of exchange rate regimes

Exchange rate regimes cover a wide possible spectrum—from free floating to various types of "hard" pegs. Under the purest free-floating regime, monetary authorities never intervene in the market and there are no—or only minimal—controls on current and capital account transactions. Hard pegs, on the other hand, can take one of three forms: a currency board, in which the domestic currency is completely backed by hard currency; dollarization, which entails the adoption of a key currency and abandonment of the domestic currency; and currency union, which means the creation of a new common currency between different countries. The free floating and hard peg regimes are regarded as the two corners (poles) of the exchange regime spectrum.

A good example of a currency board is in Hong Kong, China, where the system has been in place since the mid-1980s. The Hong Kong dollar is fixed to the United States (US) dollar, with the Special Administrative Region's foreign exchange reserves covering (more than) the total of domestic currency issued. The best known example of dollarization is in Panama, where the US dollar has long been used as legal tender, the unit of account, and medium of exchange. The best known example of a multicountry currency union is the use of the euro by a subset of European Union (EU) countries.

Between the two corners are various intermediate regimes. Closest to the hard peg is the "soft" peg fixed exchange rates. Under a hard peg, the fixed exchange rate receives institutional or legal backing that is not present under a soft peg. Next along the spectrum are various regimes that allow some kind of flexibility. A crawling peg allows slow adjustment of the exchange rate, most often to compensate for (bilateral) inflation differentials so that purchasing power parity can be maintained against a key currency. A more sophisticated way of adjusting the exchange rate is to adopt a basket peg, where the weights assigned to major currencies reflect their importance in trading relationships with the home country.

At the other corner, the differences between "clean" floating and other flexible exchange rate regimes are less straightforward. One criterion is whether central banks engage in official intervention in the foreign exchange market (buying and selling foreign exchange so as to manage the exchange rate for the domestic currency).

A fundamentalist would define free floating as the nonexistence of official intervention. With this strict criterion, however, only New Zealand (since the late 1980s) would qualify as a free floater. Others, including Frankel (volume 2), define the floating corner in terms of the absence of a target level for the exchange rate. Under this definition, an intermediate regime is characterized by the existence of a clear exchange rate target. Thus, even a regime including occasional interventions to smooth out fluctuations would be classified as floating. If interventions are carried out only to stop abrupt movements of the exchange rate or to correct clear misalignments (defined as medium-term deviations from a broadly defined equilibrium rate), the regime can be classified as floating. Under this criterion, the dollar, yen, euro, and many other developed countries' currencies are classified as floating. The dollar, yen, and euro—if the euro zone is regarded as one country—are the best known examples of floaters.

It is difficult to place countries into actual categories along this spectrum because there is a difference between what countries say they do and what they actually do regarding exchange rates. Few countries actually float, while countries classified as peggers have usually had realignments within the past 10 years. Consider first the current grouping of countries according to foreign exchange practice, using the official classification system of the International Monetary Fund (IMF).

Frankel (volume 2) attempts to count the number of countries under these categories. The fixed exchange rate camp consists of the following: 48 countries have given up an independent currency by means of a firm institutional fix, of which 12 countries are members of the European Economic and Monetary Union and 36 are from developing/transition economies. Eight countries are dollarized (Ecuador, El Salvador, Panama, four Pacific countries, and San Marino, which uses the Italian lira). Thirty-four are in monetary unions (six in the Eastern Caribbean Currency Union and 14 in the Communauté Financière Africaine franc zone); eight have currency boards (Argentina; Bosnia; Brunei Darussalam; Bulgaria; Hong Kong, China; Djibouti; Estonia; and Lithuania, with Argentina having abandoned the currency board in 2002).

The range of intermediate regimes includes 96 countries, of which 29 follow conventional soft single-currency peg arrangements and 10 have adopted basket pegs. They also include some countries that claim to be operating managed floats, but are using de facto pegs; however, even these are adjustable pegs. Forty countries are independently floating: 9 of them are industrialized countries and 31 are developing, middle-income, or transition economies.

The old policy debate

Whether the exchange rate should be fixed or floating (flexible) has long been debated. In the old days—the Bretton Woods regime to the 1980s—the debate centered on the fixed versus floating exchange rate. Milton Friedman had been a champion of floating exchange rates, even before many others had converted. However, the battle line of fixed versus floating was not the line drawn in another debate of those days, but that of monetarists versus Keynesians. Paul Krugman wrote:

> Advocates of flexible rates may be Keynesians who want to change relative prices without changing nominal wages, or monetarists who want to keep national control over the monetary aggregates. Advocates of fixed rates may be new classical economists who believe that prices are perfectly flexible and want a new monetary anchor, or interventionists who fear destabilizing speculation. (1989, pp. 96–97)

To put it differently, each of the fixed and floating regimes has benefits, of which some are valued by efficient market believers—monetarists and new classical economists—and some by market failure believers—Keynesians.

If one believes that domestic prices are sticky, as old and new Keynesians do, floating exchange rates will be attractive. Under floating exchange rates, the domestic economy can be less affected by external shocks (e.g., oil price increases for an oil importing country), in the sense that output may be stabilized. Domestic shocks, e.g., a decline in aggregate demand—would tend to result in exchange rate changes, and the impact of shocks may be mitigated by associated changes in exports and imports. This is a classical argument for flexibility of the exchange rate, with or without capital mobility.

However, this reasoning may become weaker among regionally integrated groups of countries. In the 1980s, as trade and investment barriers were lowered, some economies became significantly more integrated than before. In that setting, shocks became more symmetric. Moreover, among highly integrated economies, shocks may also be absorbed by factor mobility. This has been a traditional argument in defining an optimal currency area (OCA)—namely, a fixed exchange rate region.

With capital mobility, a fixed exchange rate regime requires the authority to follow the monetary policy of the key currency country to which the exchange rate is fixed. When capital mobility is considered essential for economic growth and autonomy of monetary policy is considered important for macroeconomic management, a floating (flexible) exchange rate regime is likely to be preferred.

A believer in the market could go a step further and reach quite a different conclusion. If prices and wages are *very* flexible (as flexible as the exchange rate), any shocks can be absorbed by domestic price and wage adjustment, and the exchange rate does not have to change. Indeed, the exchange rate *should* be fixed to provide an anchor for perfectly flexible prices. In fact, any exchange rate level is possible under these circumstances, given that prices and wages will adjust to the exchange rate. This observation can lead to a position advocating a fixed exchange rate system as a nominal "anchor," i.e., an anchor for the domestic price level.

One application of this reasoning is in the context of so-called exchange-rate-based stabilization programs. When a country is in a vicious circle of inflation and depreciation, the sudden adoption of a policy that puts defense of a fixed exchange rate at the top of the agenda and subjugates monetary and fiscal policies to that objective does stabilize the economy. Credibility of monetary policy may be restored by these means. This policy, which was often applied to transition economies and high-inflation emerging market economies in the 1980s and 1990s, often proved effective, at least in the medium term. In some cases, however, the fixed exchange rate resulted in currency crises after several years, such as what happened in Argentina and Brazil.

Support for fixed exchange rates could come from quite a different camp, on the other hand. For those who do not believe that the foreign exchange market always perfectly reflects fundamentals, floating the exchange rate is an invitation to speculation. Speculative buying and selling of foreign exchange will be a disruptive force that leaves domestic economic management difficult. This way of thinking leads to advocacy of fixed exchange rates. Table 4.1 summarizes the old debate.

Table 4.1 **Summary of Arguments for Floating and Fixed Exchange Rate Regimes**

Regime	Benefit	Reason
Floating	Absorbs external and internal shocks without changing domestic prices and wages	It is difficult and costly to change nominal prices and wages. (Keynesian)
	Retains autonomy of domestic monetary policy	Capital mobility and monetary policy autonomy are important. And fixed exchange rate is incompatible with these two elements. (market believer)
Fixed	Avoids market fluctuation by speculative attack	The foreign exchange market is not perfect and is prone to being affected by speculation. (Keynesian)
	Provides a nominal anchor	Prices and wages are so flexible that there is no equilibrium if prices, wages, and the exchange rate are all flexible. (market believer)

The role of the Asian currency crisis

If it was not clear before, the Asian currency crisis of 1997–1998—which was followed by crises in Argentina, Brazil, Russia, and Turkey—made it clear that the exchange rate regime is relevant to the overall performance of the economy. Most Asian countries adopted de facto dollar pegs before the crisis of 1997. Some countries had actually announced basket pegs, but the (econometrically estimated) weight on the dollar in the baskets tended to be high (more than 90%).[2]

The relationship between exchange rate stability and currency crises is an active topic of research. In general, managed exchange rate regimes are considered vulnerable because (i) misalignments are likely to surface eventually (e.g., due to domestic inflation, shocks affecting the country's competitiveness, or unsustainable fiscal policy); and (ii) self-fulfilling crises are always possible. Therefore, it is hard to say whether stability is better achieved via a fixed exchange rate or a free floating regime. Under fixed rates, measures should be taken to avoid the worst aspects of a currency crisis, i.e., the right policy is to "set things right" to begin with and be prepared to adjust pegs well ahead of disaster.

Before 1997, the de facto dollar peg in East Asia, given the excellent performance of the regions' economies, encouraged capital inflows, in the form of both foreign direct investment and portfolio investment. The exports of countries in the region were increasing at 15–25% in the first half of the 1990s, contributing to high economic growth. Fixed exchange rates seemed to have contributed to strong trade and investment performance among Asian emerging market economies.[3]

However, vulnerability became obvious after 1995. Since the countries in the region had a diversified trade structure, their exports tended to improve in competitiveness when the yen appreciated, but lost competitiveness when the yen depreciated. Moreover, some portfolio capital inflows were motivated by interest rate differentials in the presence of fixed exchange rates. For example, the Thai interest rate was higher than the US interest

[2] See, for example, Frankel and Wei (1994).

[3] See Ito (2000) in the Asian Development Bank study on Asian exports.

rate, while the de facto baht peg to the dollar was maintained. With the domestic economy already overheated, there was little room to lower interest rates in Thailand to discourage capital inflows. When capital flows reversed in direction, on the other hand, massive selling pressures made it impossible to maintain the exchange rate peg. In a nutshell, this was the role of exchange rate regimes in the Asian currency crisis.

This episode illustrates the problems faced by fixed exchange rates when the capital account is liberalized. Although fixed exchange rates may have advantages in encouraging trade and investment, these benefits may actually become too much of a good thing. When capital inflows cause the economy to become overheated, there is no monetary instrument to cool it down.

Given these observations, it is clear that the exchange rate regime is a central issue in groping for a new international financial architecture after the Asian currency crisis. To address it, first, the bipolar view of exchange rate regimes that has emerged in recent years will be reviewed. That will be followed by a discussion of the "impossible trinity."

The two-corner solution (bipolar view)

A bipolar view of exchange rate regimes has become prevalent since the Asian currency crisis. According to this view, the only stable exchange rate regimes are to be found at the opposite ends of the spectrum, namely, hard pegs or free floating. The reputation of currency boards, for example, was strengthened by the fact that Argentina and Hong Kong, China survived strong contagion effects during the Mexican and Asian currency crises. Some have observed that the middle ground—any exchange rate regime between the two extremes—is disappearing.[4] Others take the argument one step further by putting it in the form of a policy recommendation: the exchange rate policies of emerging economies should be induced, through IMF suggestions and program conditionality or by peer pressure, to adopt either hard pegs or floating exchange rate regimes.

---

[4] See, for example, Fischer (2001).

Dollarized economies, by definition, will not have currency crises. Several characteristics of currency boards are also supposed to make them more robust than soft pegs. First, under currency boards, capital outflows tend to reduce the circulation of the domestic currency, which raises domestic interest rates, thus inviting capital back into the country. The process is reversed for the case of capital inflows. In other words, under currency boards, monetary policy adjusts automatically to defend the fixed exchange rate. Second, fixed exchange rate regimes are most often broken due to the monetization of fiscal deficits. Under currency boards, the central bank (or currency board committee) is prohibited from buying and selling domestic debt, and, thus, from financing fiscal deficits. Third, the fact that the domestic currency is fully backed by foreign currency is reassuring for foreign investors as well as for domestic residents. This reassurance produces a dampening effect on the herd behavior that often causes liquidity shortages.

A free floating regime is considered immune to a currency crisis that arises from speculative attacks on foreign reserves, since reserves are not used to support a particular exchange rate level. Instead, free floating allows the market to find an equilibrium exchange rate in response to external and internal shocks.

However, this bipolar view is probably too simplistic on two counts. First, neither corner is completely immune to currency crises. Second, even if currency crises are less likely at the corners, extreme exchange rate regimes may not be optimal from the standpoint of national economic welfare.

Although currency boards are robust in the face of speculation by foreigners who have to borrow local currencies to sell, they are vulnerable to capital flight by domestic residents, since foreign currency backing usually extends only up to M1. Both Hong Kong, China and Argentina had foreign reserves that covered more than M1 but less than M2. Currency boards also share the problem with fixed exchange rates that when the currency is fixed against a key currency to which the country's economic links are weak, the country's export competitiveness will fluctuate as the anchor currency fluctuates against those of the country's trading partners.

The fact that the currency board of Argentina collapsed during the crises of 2001 and 2002 empirically shows that even currency boards are not immune to currency crises. The reasons for Argentina's failure are obvious. First, the peso was pegged to the dollar, despite the fact that Brazil and Europe are important trading partners of Argentina. When the Brazilian currency (the real) and the European currency (the euro) depreciated against the dollar, the Argentine trading sector was put at a competitive disadvantage. Under the fixed exchange rate system, the only way to regain competitiveness under these circumstances is through domestic price and wage deflation. This was a painful adjustment process. In addition to the problem in the trading sector, the Government relied on deficit financing. The mounting debt raised concern among investors, and they soon started to demand a higher interest rate.

Free floating regimes are also not immune to currency crises. Indeed, except for Thailand, the Asian crisis countries had floated their exchange rates before their currencies experienced severe pressures. Floating the exchange rate did not save a country if its private sector had already accumulated large external debts. The Republic of Korea (Korea) is the best example.

Thus, attacks may occur with or without fixed exchange rates. Ample reserves may be more important than the exchange rate regime. Admittedly, the fixed exchange rate may have encouraged borrowers and lenders to neglect currency risk in incurring short-term debt, and may possibly have led to excessive external debt accumulation.[5] The absence of intervention may rule out the depletion of foreign reserves, but it may cause the exchange rate to become unbearably volatile. When the exchange rate fluctuates widely, it is detrimental to trade and investment, and the volatility—especially depreciation—may bring down the government. This may be why emerging economies evince a widespread "fear of floating" (Calvo and Reinhart 2002), and why a hands-off approach toward the foreign exchange market has turned out to be neither politically nor economically feasible.

---

[5] However, it is not clear whether the exchange rate regime would have discouraged capital flows to Asia if regional exchange rates had floated much earlier.

Frankel (volume 2) describes the rise and fall of the corners hypothesis as follows. Although the bipolar (or two-corner) solution became popular immediately after the Asian crisis, its intellectual origins date back to the exchange rate mechanism (ERM) crisis of 1992–1993. Eichengreen (1994), Crockett (1994), as well as Obstfeld and Rogoff (1995) all made reference to the corners hypothesis in the context of the ERM crisis. Following the Asian crisis of 1997–1998, this hypothesis was applied to emerging markets by Summers (1999), Eichengreen (1999), and the Council on Foreign Relations. However, the corners hypothesis has always lacked a theoretical foundation. Many observers have taken it to be a corollary of the "impossible trinity" principle. The relationship between the two concepts is taken up next.

The impossible trinity

The exchange rate regime question cannot be considered and analyzed in isolation. It is related to monetary policy, capital controls, and other financial policies. Long before the Asian currency crisis, an "impossible trinity" among fixed exchange rates, capital mobility, and independent monetary policy had been acknowledged. The concept of the impossible trinity states that countries cannot simultaneously have exchange rate stability, monetary independence, or financial market integration (Table 4.2).

Since fixed exchange rates and high capital mobility mean that the interest rate of an emerging market country should be the same as that of the key currency country to which the emerging market currency is pegged, this country loses monetary policy autonomy. In this form, the trinity result explains why the Asian countries got into trouble in 1997–1998 in the first place. Capital inflows, based on the fixed exchange rate and capital account liberalization, made domestic monetary policy ineffective. Raising interest rates in order to curb inflation would have invited more capital inflows, while lowering the interest rate to discourage capital inflows would have stimulated aggregate demand. The monetary authority was clearly experiencing a dilemma. However, this was just a reflection of the well-known impossible trinity.

Table 4.2 **The Impossible Trinity**

Countries	Fixed Exchange Rate	Capital Mobility	Monetary Policy Autonomy
Precrisis Asian countries	Yes	Yes	Yes
Postcrisis Indonesia, Republic of Korea, Philippines, Singapore, Thailand	**No**	Yes	Yes
People's Republic of China, Malaysia (1998–1999)	Yes	**No**	Yes
Hong Kong, China	Yes	Yes	**No**

The People's Republic of China (PRC) and Hong Kong, China were exceptions, in that they retained fixed exchange rate regimes. The PRC maintained capital controls, so that short-term portfolio capital inflows were restricted. The PRC's regime was also strong because the current account had consistently been in surplus. On the other hand, in adopting its currency board, Hong Kong, China did not attempt to retain monetary policy independence. Prices and wages were flexible, however, allowing the domestic economy to adjust to any interest rate implied by US monetary policy.

After the crisis, Asian countries experimented with different exchange rate regimes—mostly in the form of flexible exchange rates. However, as will be discussed later, these were not free floating regimes. Countries intervened substantially, mostly to build up foreign reserves. Overall, flexible exchange rate regimes seem to have worked well in postcrisis Asia. The challenge is to decide how much flexibility is best in the future. Too much volatility would make the economy suffer from less trade and investment, while too much de facto pegging to the dollar would repeat the mistake of precrisis policy.[6]

In general, capital controls provide a third choice. They are a possible means to avoid a currency crisis as well as to maintain monetary autonomy under a fixed exchange rate. Controls on capital mobility make speculative activity more expensive, deterring speculation (thereby preventing crises), and giving authorities time to react when a crisis is under way. However,

[6] In the next section, a possible compromise in terms of a basket peg with a band will be discussed.

Frankel (volume 2) argues that, since financial markets are becoming more and more integrated, the impossible trinity really leaves us with a choice between exchange rate stability and monetary independence.

Notice, however, that the impossible trinity does not provide a theoretical foundation for the corners hypothesis, since while it may suggest that it is not possible to have *both* exchange rate stability and monetary independence, it does not rule out the possibility of having *some* of each. Theoretical support for the corners hypothesis in the form of a model has yet to be supplied.[7]

Overall, advocates of the corners hypothesis may have been overzealous. There is no theoretical reason for the choice of an optimal exchange rate regime in Asia to be constrained by the corners hypothesis. Indeed, Frankel views the Argentine crisis as having provided a severe blow to the corners hypothesis. In addition, as mentioned earlier, many developing countries in East Asia are moving back to de facto intermediate regimes.

Optimal currency areas

Given that the corners hypothesis does not constrain us from choosing only among extreme exchange rate regimes, how much fixity should the exchange rate exhibit? One approach is based on the concept of an OCA. The OCA concept was first proposed by Mundell (1961) and McKinnon (1963). They list several conditions for a group of countries to adopt a common currency or to form a currency union. The factors deemed important in determining an OCA include labor mobility (Mundell 1961), openness of the economy (McKinnon 1963), and symmetry of shocks (Bayoumi and Eichengreen 1993). The traditional view is that countries that are highly integrated with each other in trade and other economic relationships are more likely to constitute an OCA. The advantages of fixed exchange rates tend to increase with degree of economic integration, while the advantages of flexible rates decrease. Integration tends to affect openness, labor mobility,

[7] Frankel et al (2000) offer another justification for the corners hypothesis: verifiability. Simple regimes are more verifiable by market participants than band, basket, and crawl regimes.

the presence of a fiscal cushion to absorb shocks, the symmetry of shocks, and the political willingness to cooperate.

According to Frankel (volume 2) new OCA criteria emerged during the 1990s. The new criteria include a strong need to import monetary stability; a desire for further close integration with a particular neighbor or trading partner; an economy in which the foreign currency is already widely used; access to adequate reserves; an important role for the rule of law; and a strong, well-supervised, and regulated financial system.

Is the East Asian region an OCA? Lee et al (volume 2) examined whether Asia satisfies the criteria for an OCA. They found that the East Asian region has a much higher variability in output than present-day Europe. However, it would be more relevant to examine whether present-day Asia is comparable in this respect with Europe of the 1960s and 1970s, since the evolution of Asia toward economic union is probably 30–40 years behind that of Europe.

East Asia looks favorable as an OCA in terms of (i) its substantial regional trade integration, which is increasing over time; and (ii) trade structures among regional economies having become more similar over time. Another important OCA criterion, the speed of adjustment to shocks, also looks favorable in East Asia. Bayoumi and Eichengreen (1994) show that adjustments in Asia are much faster than in Europe, perhaps reflecting Asia's more flexible labor markets.

Frankel and Rose (1998, 2002) raised the possibility that country characteristics affecting the satisfaction of OCA criteria may be endogenous. Traditionally, trade and investment integration is regarded as being necessary to set up a currency union. However, when a currency union (or fixed exchange rate) is introduced, trade and investment will tend to increase.

New policy debates

The advantages of fixed and floating exchange rate regimes were reevaluated in the 1990s. Some points in the current debate are the same as those in the 1990s, but others are new, reflecting the changed international economic environment. The new debate is more complex than the old. While the three major economies—the US, the euro countries, and Japan—tend to take it for granted that their currencies will float against each other (at the same time that intraregional stability is sought within Europe), emerging markets have become a focus of attention. The benefits and costs of alternative regimes as they appear in the new policy debate are discussed. The upshot, as a knowledgeable observer has concluded, is that "no single exchange rate regime is right for all countries or at all times" (Frankel 1999).

The advantages of fixed exchange rates in the new debate can be summarized as follows: fixed exchange rates (i) provide an effective nominal anchor for monetary policy and thus represent a more credible commitment to fight inflation; expectations of low inflation mean that workers and firms set wages and prices accordingly, bringing lower inflation at a given level of output; (ii) encourage trade and investment by reducing uncertainty and transactions costs; (iii) preclude competitive devaluations; and (iv) avoid speculative bubbles.

On the other hand, the advantages of floating exchange rates can be summarized as follows: floating exchange rates (i) allow a country to conduct an independent monetary policy; (ii) allow automatic adjustments to trade shocks, since the currency responds to adverse developments even in the face of sticky domestic prices or wages; (iii) allow a country to retain seigniorage and a lender-of-last-resort capability;[8] (iv) avoid speculative attacks (under a fixed rate, it can be politically difficult to change the exchange rate peg, so countries may tend to wait too long to abandon targets when there is a major reversal of capital flows); and (v) discourage currency mismatches in the balance sheets of domestic firms and financial institutions (when an exchange rate is fixed, there may be a tendency to have high unhedged exposure to foreign currencies, because firms and banks foolishly underestimate the possibility of a future break in the currency value).

Many of these arguments—on both sides of the debate—are controversial. For example, the absence of central bank credibility

[8] Argentina's experience shows that even countries that move to a firm fix and allow foreign bank entry will need a lender of last resort.

may appear to suggest the use of a fixed exchange rate as a nominal anchor. However, at the same time, the presence of credibility may allow the fixed exchange rate to operate without a problem. Moreover, the value of a fixed exchange rate as a nominal anchor can be overstated, as there are other possible nominal anchors in addition to exchange rate pegs (monetarism, a gold standard, inflation targeting, and nominal income targeting). Any nominal anchor provides support for preventing excessive money growth. To further complicate this picture, each candidate for nominal anchor has its own vulnerability: exogenous fluctuations in any anchor will create fluctuations in monetary conditions that may not be positively correlated with the needs of the economy.

Along the same lines, highly open countries may find it beneficial to have a stable exchange rate for trade and investment promotion, since damage to imports and exports from exchange rate fluctuations are likely to be larger in an economy with a higher trade/gross domestic product (GDP) ratio.[9] Thus, if a small open economy trades with a large economy almost exclusively, then the former may indeed find it beneficial to fix its currency to the latter. However, if the small country has many diversified trading partners, then it may prefer to fix the currency to a basket of major currencies. Moreover, even in the latter case, if enough hedging instruments—forward contracts, derivatives, etc.—are available, the exchange rate risk may be alleviated, so that a floating exchange rate regime may be justified.

Similar qualifications can be offered for arguments in support of floating rates. For example, while they may safeguard monetary autonomy in principle, the unfortunate reality is that few developing countries have been able to make effective use of discretionary monetary policy. Moreover, floating rates may not be effective in helping adjustment if pass-through of imported prices is high. With a high level of pass-through, the cost of depreciation in terms of domestic inflation becomes high. Again, however, things are more complicated than this. For example, the pass-through ratio may be endogenous to the exchange rate

[9] However, this statement may be qualified in an economy such as Hong Kong, China, where many imports are reexported after some manufacturing value is added.

regime. That is, under a floating exchange rate regime, importers and distributors may get used to exchange rate fluctuations and become wiser in hedging exchange rate risk, or may become patient in smoothing out exchange rate fluctuations. Floating rates do not necessarily provide fail-safe protection against extreme forms of instability, since overvaluation, excessive volatility, and crashes are possible in either fixed or floating regimes. Last, the argument that floating rates discourage currency exposure has weaknesses. Specifically, if banks and firms are irrational, countries would be better-off introducing exchange rate volatility just to deter borrowers from incurring unhedged dollar liabilities, so that foreigners are unwilling to take open positions in currencies of emerging markets.

Table 4.3 may summarize the fixed versus floating exchange rate debate. Note that it is not necessarily easier to resolve these arguments when focusing on a concrete case. To illustrate, it can be argued that the importance of trade in Asia creates a presumption that exchange rate volatility and risk are more disruptive there than in other regions, suggesting a case for exchange rate pegs.[10] However, while the empirical literature indeed supports the belief that exchange rate volatility matters for trade, it suggests that the effect is small, so economies can tolerate volatility without major damage to international trade. Also, major destinations and origins of trade of Asian countries included US, Japan, and Europe. The dollar, yen, and euro float against one another, making single-currency pegs less attractive. Only a basket peg could confer stability, but in view of the growing importance of intraregional trade, these pegs would have to be identical across countries. Moreover, the case for pegging has become weaker, because hedging is now easier. At the same time, the argument for floating is becoming stronger: exchange rate flexibility in response to changing competitive pressures now seems to matter most for market perceptions.

Or consider the case for pegging in Asia from the perspective of financial markets development. Asian financial markets are

[10] Eichengreen (1999) considers studies on exchange rate volatility and foreign direct investment as less conclusive. In any case, however, future growth for Asia will depend increasingly on domestic demand.

Table 4.3 **Benefits and Costs of Fixed and Floating Exchange Rate Regimes**

Regime	Benefits	Costs (and rebuttal)
A. Fixed Exchange Rate (soft peg) Kept at a constant value of a major key currency by official interventions and other policies, especially monetary policy (cf Frankel, McKinnon)	Provides a nominal anchor, a credible commitment to fight inflation	
	Avoids speculative bubbles (asset price inflation)	
	Encourages trade and investment, due to reduced transaction costs and currency risk	Hedge for currency risk is possible (hedge is expensive).
	Precludes competitive devaluation	It may invite speculative attack.
B. Floating Exchange Rate Determined by the market, without official interventions. The exchange rate level or change is not included in an objective function of policies, especially monetary policy (cf Eichengreen, Frankel)	Can attain capital mobility and domestic policy autonomy	
	Retains the seigniorage and lender-of-last resort function	Capital flows may cause too much volatility of exchange rate.
		Nominal anchor is lost (but inflation targeting would do).
	Adjusts automatically to trade shocks	Fluctuations of the exchange rate may hurt trade and investment.
	Avoids speculative attack to the fixed rate	Misalignment and overshooting may occur.

underdeveloped. There is some evidence that more stable exchange rates mean countries find it less expensive to borrow abroad and encourage residents to hold bank deposits denominated in domestic currency, encouraging the development of financial markets. But there is also evidence that pegged rates are a source of fragility that undermines the ability of financial markets to allocate resources efficiently. As noted earlier, by pegging the exchange rate, the government provides a guarantee against currency risk, thus encouraging unhedged borrowing. When the peg inevitably collapses, unhedged firms suffer financial distress.

Pros and cons of alternative exchange rate regimes

Arguments for a basket exchange rate regime

In view of the ambiguities, some economists have argued for a regime that attempts to strike a compromise between fixed and floating exchange rates. A band system based on a basket of currencies was proposed by Williamson (2000), Ito et al (1998), and Ogawa et al (volume 2), among others. Under a basket peg, the exchange rate of a country is determined as a weighted average of the bilateral exchange rates of trading partners. Weights are chosen to minimize a loss function. For example, Ito et al (1998) proposed minimizing the volatility of trade surpluses. The "band" aspect of such a regime means that there is a tolerance band around the central rate determined from the basket.

The basket band regime is inherently a compromise between fixed and floating exchange rates. The regime is aimed at allowing flexibility of the exchange rate as an adjustment mechanism to various idiosyncratic shocks, while it does not allow speculative attacks or misalignment. The basket band regime allows monetary autonomy to the extent that it does not conflict with the exchange rate band. However, these features could invite criticism from both right and left of the exchange rate regime spectrum: fixed rate purists (no band) and floating rate fundamentalists (no intervention, no target).

The benefits of a currency basket regime include the stabilization of trade competitiveness by stabilizing real effective exchange rates. Since countries have many export destinations and many competitors, a currency basket would stabilize trade competitiveness better than pegging to a single currency. Ito et al

(1998) show that the adoption of a de facto dollar peg by Asian countries even though their trade weight with Japan was substantial was one of the most significant factors that contributed to the 1997 crisis. As the yen depreciated against the dollar in 1995–1997, the real effective exchange rate of Asian countries appreciated, reducing export competitiveness and increasing current account deficits.

Another benefit from a basket band currency regime is related to its effect on capital flows. Ogawa and Sun (2001) show that the responsiveness of capital flows to foreign exchange risk against the dollar is much larger than the responsiveness of capital flows to exchange risk against the yen. Since a currency basket (rather than a de facto dollar peg) would have increased the exchange risk against the dollar, a currency basket system would have depressed capital inflows into Korea and Thailand. Sasaki (2002) also shows that the de facto dollar peg induced more capital inflows into Korea, Malaysia, Philippines, Singapore, and Thailand than a currency basket or floating exchange rate regime would have done. Analyzing the types of capital inflows, Sasaki (2002) also found that the effects of variable dollar exchange rates were greater for bank liabilities than for portfolio investment or foreign direct investment.

While the adoption of a common basket band regime by East Asian countries may yield important benefits, there would also be costs. First, a currency basket is not crisis-proof. Advocates of floating exchange rate regimes such as Fischer (2001) emphasize that soft pegs such as a currency basket are crisis-prone and not viable in the long run. However, as argued above, no exchange rate regime is crisis-proof. Second, nontransparency may be a significant shortcoming.[11] Calculating optimal weights for a currency basket can be difficult, and interventions can be technically complex. This being so, it may be difficult for market participants to verify that monetary authorities are indeed following the basket regime. Williamson (2000a), who himself proposed an intermediate basket band regime, admitted that such a regime may lack

[11] Frankel et al (2000) point out that a simple peg or float is easier to verify and therefore to monitor than a more complicated intermediate regime.

transparency. It can be difficult for the public to evaluate policy decisions. Third, basket band regimes may preclude some types of policy cooperation, and—most seriously—they lack a clear announcement of the parameters guiding the management of the exchange rate. Fourth, advocates of fixed exchange rates criticize the basket band approach on the ground that it lacks a nominal anchor. For example, Mussa et al (2000) point out that since the late 1980s, many developing countries have successfully controlled high inflation with exchange rate stabilization. However, it is obvious that not all countries face this challenge. And for those that do, exchange-rate-based stabilization has not proven to be a panacea. Countries that have used exchange-rate-based stabilization have tended to become dependent on international capital markets and are therefore vulnerable to sudden reversals of capital flows. Further, exiting from a hard peg can be difficult.[12]

The benefits and costs of a basket regime are summarized in Table 4.4. These benefits and costs are based on the consideration of a "generic" basket-band system. But much depends on the specific characteristics of the regime as applied in given circumstances, i.e., on the weights assigned to different currencies in the basket, on the width of the band, on the disclosure of the basket and band, and on the rigidity with which the edge of the band is defended.

Suppose a group of countries with diversified trading partners recognizes that a currency basket regime is desirable. There are still some complications in implementing a basket system. First, the inertia associated with the use of the dollar as a key currency is strong. Although other currencies can compete with the dollar as a store of value, the dollar will remain the key currency as long as it retains its function as a medium of exchange.[13] Second, the relationship between a basket band exchange rate regime and monetary policy is unclear. If the band is too narrow, the common

[12] Some argue that, in addition to nontransparency, basket regimes suffer from the additional shortcoming that the intervention strategy becomes complex, because authorities may need to intervene in many currencies. But this is clearly not true. The intervention currency can be any one currency to achieve the desirable basket peg value.

[13] Several studies by Ogawa et al (volume 2), for example, have shown that the dollar retained its position in the international monetary system after the introduction of the euro.

Table 4.4 **Benefits and Costs of a Basket Peg Regime**[a]

Benefits	Costs
Fewer fluctuations in trade balances (or gross domestic product fluctuations), compared with soft peg	Not crisis-proof (less chance of misalignment, but not perfect; could lose foreign reserves)
Moderate capital flows. Adds some currency risk to prevent a "one-way bet" (risk of being attacked is smaller than in fixed exchange rate regime)	No transparency, and calculation of the basket may be too complicated
Adds flexibility in managing external shocks (compared with a fixed exchange rate regime)	Not completely flexible (compared with the floating exchange rate regime)
Gives some anchor to prevent misalignment (compared with a floating exchange rate regime)	Loses a nominal anchor (compared with the fixed exchange rate regime), leading to possibly higher risk premium of interest rate
Adopts similar baskets in the region, so that regional currencies with strong trade ties appreciate and depreciate together	Precludes policy coordination among the neighboring countries (solving coordination failure, Ogawa and Ito [2002])
Preconditions: (i) ability to manage (independent) monetary policy prudently when countering external and internal shocks, without nominal anchor (possibly with inflation targeting); (ii) fiscal policy prudence; (iii) credibility in macroeconomic management	

[a] A reference central rate is the value of the dollar, yen, and euro with weights. The exchange rate is kept in the vicinity of the central rate (with an announced or unannounced tolerance band). Coordination with neighboring countries is needed (cf Ogawa et al, volume 2).

criticism of fixed rate regimes would apply: namely, the loss of monetary policy autonomy. On the other hand, if the band is too wide, then a common criticism of floating rates would apply: the loss of a nominal anchor. Last, there may be a problem of coordination failure in case a band is adopted by more than two countries.

A basket band regime is not necessarily incompatible with other monetary policy goals, such as inflation targeting. It is sometimes argued that with a currency band and inflation targeting, there would be too many goals with a limited set of policy instruments, basically approaching the impossible trinity. However, Ogawa et al (volume 2) show that, in the face of several conceivable shocks, a managed exchange rate regime will be compatible with inflation targeting. For example, an exogenous currency appreciation shock will lower inflation via dampened demand from a slump in tradables and lower import prices. Both the basket band and inflation targeting will prescribe a lower interest rate (to encourage capital outflows and combat deflationary pressure). Alternatively, a domestic inflation shock caused by an increase in aggregate demand would increase domestic prices and, thus, reduce exporters' competitiveness, impacting trade balances and depreciating the currency. This situation will call for a tighter monetary policy, both to achieve the inflation target and to keep the currency within the band. Last, an adverse supply shock (drought, destruction of productive capacity) will increase prices and reduce output. The exchange rate will likely depreciate due to current account deficits and lower output. Again, there would be no conflict between the basket band regime and inflation targeting, although output fluctuations would be large in this case.

On coordination, if one country switches from a dollar peg to a currency basket while others remain on the dollar peg, the first mover may face increased fluctuations in price competitiveness and therefore trade balances (if, for example, the dollar depreciates against the yen). Ogawa and Ito (2002) analyze coordination failure in choosing an exchange rate system in a two-country game theoretic model. Only if both monetary authorities coordinate to adopt the optimal currency basket peg at the same time will the optimal currency basket regime be implemented. Coordination failure is more likely if monetary authorities are risk averse, so monetary authorities need to coordinate their exchange rate policies. Creating a common currency basket that monetary authorities make reference to in setting exchange rate policy will prevent competitive devaluations.

To deal with coordination failure, a common basket has been proposed. Although the optimal basket may be different from one country to another, if the band is wide enough and the fluctuations among the major currencies are small enough, then adopting a common basket may be close enough to optimal, automatically achieving coordination. Indeed, if the band around the common peg becomes narrow enough, through convergence of the economies and increasing intraregional trade, then the common basket can become a common currency. This is analogous to a transition from the ECU to the euro in Europe.

Arguments for monetary union

Exchange rate stability may be the most important benefit of monetary union (Table 4.5). Recent empirical evidence shows that exchange rate stability promotes commerce and will therefore boost trade (Pozo 1992, Rose 2000, Helliwell 1998). The evidence is particularly strong that currency unions reduce trading costs. Alesina and Barro (2002) model the fact that a common currency reduces the costs of trading across borders and thereby stimulates the volume of international trade. Rose (2000) demonstrates empirically that sharing a common money increases the volume of bilateral trade dramatically.

Table 4.5 **Benefits and Costs of Monetary Union**

Benefits	Costs
Exchange rate stability (in a union) to promote trade and investment	
Central bank independence led by the leading country's central bank	Central bank autonomy is lost, except in the leading country.
Peer pressure for macroeconomic policy coordination	Asymmetric shocks cause difficulty without capital mobility and fiscal cross-border transfers.
Preconditions: High intraunion trade, symmetric shocks, factor mobility, price and wage flexibility, policy coordination	

Source: Wyplosz (2002).

Monetary union may also promote macroeconomic stability more broadly, however. Alesina and Barro (2002) note that a currency union commits clients to a stable monetary policy and generally provides a better commitment device than a fixed exchange rate regime. Beyond this, a country's macroeconomic policies become of common interest to the other members of the union, so there is peer pressure to impose sound macroeconomic policies that are not captive to local politics. There is also some indication of wage and price moderation under some monetary unions, which is known to "work to the benefit of all interested parties" (Kydland and Prescott 1977).

Last, Hausmann et al (2000) argued that currency unions can help developing countries by increasing access to long-term financing. If dollarization lowers the variability of relative prices between the home country and the US (for example), then long-term financing in a dollarized regime would be less risky than in other regimes. The empirical evidence suggests that currency unions increase the co-movement of prices among participating countries, giving weight to this argument.

As for the costs of currency unions, the key one is, of course, that countries belonging to a monetary union are forced to have an independent monetary policy. Alesina and Barro (2002) note that with an independent monetary policy, the monetary authority can offset exogenous real disturbances by engineering high or low inflation. The OCA theory points out that, in the absence of independent monetary policy, asymmetric shocks will cause difficulties unless labor markets are flexible and/or labor can move freely across the currency area. A key criterion for an OCA, consequently, has been taken to be labor mobility or real wage flexibility.[14]

However, the costs of losing independent monetary policy can be overstated. First, these costs depend on the incidence of asymmetric shocks, i.e., on the extent of co-movement of output and prices with the anchor country. The loss is smaller if greater co-movement translates into price stability in the client country. But this occurs only if relative prices do not vary significantly between the countries. Similarity in production structure tends to reduce the variability of relative output and prices across countries. Low transaction costs for international trade in goods and services and a high degree of mobility in production also reduce the variability of relative prices. Moreover, there is evidence that the existence of a currency union itself raises the co-movement of prices. The evidence on co-movement of output is less clear.

Second, even when asymmetric shocks are important, it is not clear that countries make good use of their monetary policy independence. Calvo and Reinhart (2002) and Hausmann et al (2000)

[14] Europe's labor markets are rigid and labor mobility is low, for example, so one potential cost to monetary union in the euro area is that the monetary policy may be ill-suited to addressing countries' idiosyncratic shocks. Using a Taylor rule to estimate what policies would have been adopted in each country without monetary union, however, Wyplosz (2002) shows that although this has been an issue in Europe, the cost has been low (the difference from "ideal" Taylor rule policies has been negligible in many countries).

for example, argue that, in practice, countries tend to follow procyclical monetary policies.[15]

Last, the cost of losing monetary policy independence can be attenuated through the design of appropriate mechanisms within the monetary union. For example, accommodations by the anchor country and seigniorage revenue sharing can be arranged. Alesina and Barro (2002) show that accommodative monetary policy by the anchor country (to shocks in client countries) can be mutually beneficial if they take into account the relative sizes of the two economies and if there is some form of compensation flow from client to anchor. One source of compensation could be the seigniorage income that accrues to the anchor country when client countries hold the anchor country's currency. One possibility would be for the anchor country to provide the initial stock of anchor currency needed to get the system going, and for the client country to "pay back" with the present value of the flows needed to continue using the anchor country's currency.

Monetary unions may also have other disadvantages beyond the loss of monetary autonomy. For example, they must include fiscal constraints, which are inevitably arbitrary.[16] Monetary unions may also make it more difficult for monetary and fiscal policies to be coordinated.[17] Last, transfers of sovereignty may go beyond just monetary policy into areas of taxation and labor policy.

Dollar peg and dollarization

McKinnon (volume 2) has argued that East Asia may find it advisable to explicitly adopt a dollar peg. His argument is based mostly on the benefits of lowering transaction costs and taking advantage of the dollar standard that has been emerging. It can be regarded as advocating a monetary union not only in East Asia, but also between the region and the US. Therefore, the test to distinguish between monetary union and dollar peg is whether

[15] However, Broda (2001) finds that countries with floating regimes demonstrate better economic performance in the face of exogenous shocks to the terms of trade.

[16] In Europe they are also probably excessively restrictive (deficits may not exceed 3% of GDP).

[17] There is not much coordination across countries regarding fiscal policy in Europe, nor between Europe's monetary (President of the European Central Bank) and fiscal (Chair of the Council of Ministers of Economics and Finance [ECOFIN]) authorities.

East Asia constitutes an OCA with the US. The benefits and costs of the dollar peg are summarized in Table 4.6.

Barro (volume 2) examined the issue of which currency should be the anchor currency for various countries in the world. Countries with (i) little ability to commit to low inflation, (ii) lots of trade with a potential anchor country, and (iii) high price and output co-movements with the potential anchor country are the most natural participants in a currency union. Based on these criteria, there seems to be a natural dollar area involving Canada, Mexico, most of Central America, and parts of South America (excluding Argentina and Brazil). But the dollar zone seems to also encompass some Asian countries: Hong Kong, China; Philippines; and Singapore. These Asian economies trade more with the US and are closely associated with the US business cycle. Such an analysis, however, is based on historical data. In reality, the decision of whether or not to join a currency union should be based on inflation, trade, and co-movement of prices and output that would apply *after* entry.

Table 4.6 **Benefits and Costs of the Dollar Peg**

Benefits	Costs
It is an efficient medium of exchange (lower transactions costs).	It would be better if the currency is united like the euro (by single currency).
It provides a nominal anchor; adopts US monetary policy; low inflation is achieved.	If a country does not satisfy the OCA test, the economy suffers from asymmetric shocks.
It can be carried out unilaterally by a small economy. But regional cooperation is automatically achieved if all peg to the US dollar. Seigniorage is retained (as opposed to the domestic use of the dollar).	
With Japan joining the dollar bloc, the region would be stabilized optimally. East Asian part of the dollar standard would be formed.	
Currency attack would be weaker, contagion would be contained, and a long-term bond market without large premium would be possible.	
Preconditions: (i) History is important. The dollar (not the euro, nor the yen) has already become a central currency. (ii) Recommended for a country with persistent inflation, financial instability, and currency crises.	

OCA = optimum currency area.
Source: Wyplosz (2002).

Exchange rate coordination and monetary cooperation in Asia

In the immediate postcrisis period, several Asian countries adopted floating exchange rates. While the period of de facto relatively free floating was brief, as will be explained below, many of these economies continue to describe their exchange rate systems as floating rates (important exceptions are PRC; Hong Kong, China; and Malaysia). The question thus arises: is floating now incompatible with monetary unification later?

The answer seems to be that it is not, for two reasons. First, there is a case for cooperation even when countries float with an inflation target. Cooperation and institution building can be based on financial sector development issues rather than on monetary policy or exchange rates. Developing financial markets and strengthening supervision and regulation are the key tasks facing the Asian region at present, and there may be substantial scope for cooperation on these issues (see Eichengreen [volume 2] as well as Girardin [volume 2]). Accordingly, Eichengreen (volume 2) suggests the creation of an Asian Financial Institute on the platform of the Association of Southeast Asian Nations (ASEAN)+3. This institute would promote financial stability and development in the region; provide technical assistance to national agencies seeking to strengthen prudential supervision and regulation; and run training programs for bank inspectors, securities and exchange commissioners, and accountants.

Eichengreen (volume 2) asserts that improvement in the soundness of financial institutions and systems will enhance the stability and efficiency of financial markets in the region. In turn, stable and efficient financial markets may contribute to the stability of nominal and real exchange rates. Whether financial stability is sufficient for exchange rate stability is certainly questionable, as many studies have found that exchange rate volatility cannot be explained by changes in fundamentals. But if financial stability is at least conducive to exchange rate stability, the Eichengreen proposal is easily seen as a step that increases the feasibility of a future monetary union.

Second, the period during which Asian currencies were managed very flexibly was relatively brief in the wake of the Asian currency crisis (late 1997–early 1998). Several observers have noted that since 1999, many Asian currencies have tended to go back to de facto dollar pegs, as was the case before the 1997 Thai devaluation. The reason is that many Asian countries seem to suffer from "fear of floating." That is, they regard extreme volatility in the exchange rate—and this view is supported by empirical evidence—to be harmful to trade and investment.

It follows that those countries in the region that trade heavily with each other are likely to find it more conducive to economic growth in the near term to have stable currency relationships among themselves. And, indeed, many observers have found that Asia has large intraregional trade and investment ratios.[18] The fact that intraregional trade has been increasing and has reached a level that is comparable to that within the euro area has led some researchers and policymakers to conclude that the East Asian region passes the OCA test. If so, it follows that countries in the region may be better-off if they coordinate in managing their exchange rates.

Thus, the next question is how to establish "stable" currency relationships, and to which currency stability they should be linked. The de facto dollar pegs that seem to have emerged in the region more recently would tend to promote stability in intraregional exchange rates. However, these de facto dollar pegs are deficient in other respects. Specifically, Asian countries trade in significant proportions with US, Japan, Europe, and neighboring countries—with some variations among the countries. This implies that to maintain trade competitiveness, stability of

[18] For example, Lee et al (volume 2) examine various economic conditions for currency union in Asia. On the trade side, the nine Asian countries in their sample are found to show intraregional trade much like Europe. It should be noted that this is despite the fact that, compared with North America and Europe, the Asian region is behind in moving toward regional cooperation. Until a few years ago, Japan and Korea were the only two countries in the Organisation for Economic Co-operation and Development (OECD) that did not have any preferential trade arrangements. It was only recently that Japan signed its first free trade agreement with Singapore. Regional cooperation on the financial front seems to be proceeding before cooperation in the trade area in Asia.

the real effective exchange rate is important, rather than simply bilateral stability vis-à-vis the dollar. Therefore, exchange rate management should be focused on some sort of basket currency value, with varying weights on the dollar, yen, and euro. This has led some observers to propose the use of currency baskets as exchange rate pegs for countries in the region (Williamson 1999, 2000b; Ito et al 1998). Under this proposal, each Asian country would calculate an optimal basket in order to stabilize its real effective exchange rate, with all other Asian exchange rates as is.

One of the problems in calculating the optimal exchange rate in this manner, however, is that, as emphasized above, Asian countries trade increasingly with each other. Since neighboring countries' exchange rates have large weights in each other's real effective exchange rates, their exchange rate policies cannot be ignored. For example, suppose that an Asian country—say Thailand—trades with US, Japan, Europe, and a neighbor—say Malaysia—in equal proportions. Taking those trade shares as given, each currency has a weight of one fourth in Thailand's currency basket. But, of course, Malaysia would be doing the same thing. Suppose that for some reason, Malaysia adopts a dollar peg. Then, for Thailand the weight of the dollar (zone) trading partners increases from 25% to 50%. In this case, the Thai baht will behave more like a dollar-peg country, even though the US is not a dominant trading partner. But Thailand would behave more like a euro-peg country if Malaysia adopted the euro, and like a yen-peg country if Malaysia adopted the yen. Therefore, decisions of trade-linked countries about exchange rate regimes depend on each other, and there is an obvious gain from coordination. This was argued in Ogawa and Ito (2002).

A common basket, or a common currency (value), for the region would solve the coordination problem. Therefore, a step further than idiosyncratic basket band pegs would be adopting a common regional basket. Wyplosz (2002) sees this as a desirable development. He reviews the European experience to draw lessons for Asia and proposes the creation of an Asian monetary system based on an Asian currency unit (ACU).

However, implementing such a system has certain prerequisites. Specifically, exchange rate coordination requires macroeconomic policy coordination enforced by peer pressure. If policy coordination fails and economic fundamentals are not consistent with exchange rate stability, intraregional exchange rate stability becomes impossible. Monetary cooperation in the form of exchange rate coordination thus calls for economic dialogue and surveillance in the region. Asian countries have lacked such a forum for a long time. However, the ASEAN+3 framework is now developing the mechanisms for economic surveillance. Whether it works like a similar mechanism among the advanced countries—G7, OECD, and Council of Ministers of Economics and Finance in the EU—remains to be seen.

On the other hand, when fundamentals are right in a coordinated exchange rate arrangement (i.e., when the fundamentals are consistent with stable currency values), but the market acts incorrectly, there is scope for concerted actions from policymakers, possibly in the form of intervention. For this purpose, it is helpful for countries coordinating their exchange rate policies to have a scheme in place for financial assistance and monetary cooperation to maintain exchange rate stability. In East Asia, the swap agreements under the Chiang Mai Initiative (CMI) are thus a potentially important step forward in making it possible to strengthen exchange rate coordination.[19] Under the CMI, swap agreements can be used to obtain hard currency (in exchange for local currencies) in times of acute financial difficulties. However, the current arrangement may be inadequate to really support intraregional exchange rate stability. First, the financial resources committed—either under the mutual swaps among the ASEAN countries or the bilateral swaps between one of the "plus three" countries and the ASEAN countries—are insufficient to be effective. Second, for the arrangement to help stabilize regional exchange rates, regional surveillance would need to be enhanced.

[19] Wyplosz (2002), for example, clearly sees the CMI as an important step toward integration beyond idiosyncratic baskets.

Because even very large amounts of financing would not be enough if exchange rates are fundamentally misaligned, any financial cooperation should be backed by sound macroeconomic policies ensured by surveillance.

When enough trust in the surveillance process is generated, swap arrangements can be replaced by reserve pooling (Chaipravat, this volume). To determine whether financial assistance is extended from a reserve pooling arrangement, a judgment has to be made to determine whether a country is facing a liquidity crisis, possibly induced by contagion, or a solvency crisis driven by fundamental weaknesses within the domestic economy. IMF—and to a lesser extent the World Bank and the regional development banks—has acted as the sole agency in such a mechanism. However, the Asian crisis showed that the resources at IMF may not be enough, and that IMF prescriptions for responding to economic crises may benefit from inputs from the region.

The common currency unit should therefore have three pillars: surveillance, financing, and an ERM. This point is emphasized both by Wyplosz (2002) and by Lee et al (volume 2). Enhancing the CMI will thus be an important step toward the common currency goal.

The likely scenario is thus that the exchange rate regime discussion, in parallel with financial cooperation and strong surveillance, will lead the Asian region to a currency union—i.e., the basket exchange rate system or the Asian monetary system will become an intermediate step toward a currency union in the region. Economic conditions, such as those concerning the level of intraregional trade and the extent of co-movement among macroeconomic variables, will have to be there to justify the choice of exchange rate regime. Despite the increase in intraregional trade and improvement in policy dialogues and coordination, Asia at present does not satisfy many economic criteria for a successful currency union. But some degree of economic integration is endogenous to the choice of the exchange rate regime. That is, causality may run from currency union to trade and general economic integration. Recent empirical studies suggest that creation of a common currency area (CCA) even for a group of countries with diverse economic backgrounds and exposed to asymmetric shocks could lead to the expansion of trade and synchronization of business cycles across the countries belonging to the group.[20]

A fundamental difficulty in Asia is that there is no consensus on where the common regional currency arrangement will end up. In the case of EU-accessing countries—the Baltic states, Czech Republic, Hungary, and Poland—they are quite sure that they will achieve "euro-rization" in the end. Therefore, questions on the appropriate exchange rate system are only about their intermediate steps. In Asia, however, the end state itself is not agreed upon. There are indeed many obstacles to monetary unification across Asia: (i) Asian economies are heterogeneous; (ii) Asian economies may trade less with one another than do other entities that form part of monetary unions; (iii) Asia lacks Europe's integrationist tradition; and (iv) outside powers (US) are not supportive of the movement. There are various options in responding to these difficulties: (i) a monetary union among ASEAN countries only, (ii) a Greater China monetary union, and (iii) a monetary union between Japan and Korea. But each proposal has obstacles and, overall, an Asian monetary union is a distant prospect.

A second complicating factor affecting the ultimate destination of this process is that, according to many, monetary union will be a political decision. The countries of the North American Free Trade Agreement (NAFTA)—Canada, Mexico, US—may find themselves satisfying the currency union criteria, but they have not moved to a currency union because that does not have political appeal. On the other hand, 30 years ago Europe was hardly an ideal candidate for a CCA, but it has become united through political will. One important lesson of the European experience with monetary unification is that formation of a currency union is essentially a political process.

[20] Rose and Engel (2001) show that members of a currency union tend to trade more among themselves and experience a lower degree of volatility of real exchange rates than countries with their own monies. Business cycles are more synchronized across currency union members than across noncurrency union countries. Rose and van Wincoop (2001) leave little doubt that national money is a barrier to international trade. They estimate that trade barriers associated with national borders are halved when countries join a currency union.

We are skeptical that in Asia at this moment, political will exists for monetary union, or a single currency. One of the important reasons for this is that the PRC and Japan—the two countries that are expected to provide leadership in bringing Asian countries together for monetary and financial integration—have not been able to agree on many economic issues. However, it is possible that regional economic integration may induce friendlier relationships among the countries in the region in the near future. What is crucial for political commitment in the region will be a unified vision for the future shared by PRC, Japan, and Korea, as well as the ASEAN countries. With a commonly shared vision, the monetary authorities in East Asia are likely to seek ways to cooperate on their exchange rate regimes. From this perspective, if the East Asian countries realize political as well as economic advantages of belonging to—and subsequently agree to establish—a currency union, then the diversity of their exchange rate regimes may not pose an obstacle that is as serious as it now appears.

Given these constraints to exchange rate policy coordination in Asia, a realistic strategy for monetary integration would be to search for a sequencing of regime changes from the current state of diverse systems on the way to creating a CCA. However, in promoting a successful CCA, political agreements alone would not suffice, unless they are manifested in actual coordination of financial and exchange rate policies. To this end, a sequencing of regime changes in which a series of steps could be taken over five stages is proposed. The stages are described in the next section.

Synthesis and policy recommendations

From the trends described in the last section, we expect that, in the long run, Asia will head toward some form of exchange rate coordination, and possibly a currency union. Globalization in trade and finance is likely to necessitate the reduction of the number of currencies in the world, and Asia will not be an exception. However, it is recognized that the process to currency union is likely to be a long and uncertain one. Also, whether a single currency in the region will be established, much like the euro, or whether the region would be linked to the dollar is debatable. Even if a euro-like currency emerges in Asia, whether the yen becomes a part of it or stays outside a non-Japan Asian currency area is uncertain. What is observed now cannot be taken as a given since, as emphasized at the end of the last section, many economic and political conditions are endogenous to the process.

Stage one: expanding and consolidating the CMI

Efforts to introduce a collective regional exchange rate system are likely to be futile at this stage. The existing variety of exchange rate systems, however, would not necessarily interfere with the integration process. In the short run, therefore, this variety should be accepted. However, progress can be made in the meantime through more transparent and perhaps coordinated intervention in foreign exchange markets, coordination on financial sector reform issues, and enhanced trade integration.

Nonsystematic intervention that is not explicit about the purpose or the point of intervention among the Asian floaters creates uncertainties concerning exchange rate policy in these countries, thereby inhibiting stabilizing speculation. Intervention should be transparent enough to inform other countries in the region what their partners are doing in terms of exchange rate policy. This transparency together with similar modes of intervention would promote cooperation on exchange rate policy. Only when members of the CMI succeed in building trust among themselves with regard to policy coordination and learn to cooperate would they be able to develop economic and political conditions favorable for introducing a collective exchange rate system.

Out of sheer necessity, for instance, officials of the ministries of finance of PRC, Japan, and Korea have been holding informal (or sometimes formal) meetings for policy coordination. In response to the recent appreciation of the yen, which has also strengthened the value of the Korean won vis-à-vis the dollar, the finance officials from the three countries are reported to have considered joint intervention in their respective foreign exchange markets. This is an encouraging sign, suggesting that there has been considerable improvement in the climate for policy coordination in East Asia. Finance ministry and central bank officials of ASEAN+3 also point out that they have been able to discuss a wide range of regional as well as bilateral policy issues with greater depth and frequency than before the inception of the CMI, as they have come to know each other personally. The close interactions among the CMI countries have helped create a network of East Asian policymakers to open various channels of formal and informal policy dialogues.

Region-wide efforts directed at reforming the financial systems of individual East Asian countries would enable the region as a whole to defend itself better against financial shocks. Together with these efforts, building regional capital markets should also be an integral part of the regional financial integration process. The efficient functioning of regional capital markets requires a financial infrastructure that includes regional credit agencies, clearing and settlement systems, mechanisms for cross-border securities borrowing and lending, credit enhancement and guarantee agencies, and trading systems. Countries participating in the integration process should also initiate discussion of harmonization of standards, legal and regulatory systems, and tax treatment of cross-border financial flows.

Last, PRC and Japan have expressed their interest in negotiating free trade agreements with other members of the CMI group. They also realize that stabilizing bilateral exchange rates of the regional currencies would help in their negotiations. This development, together with the lingering fear of another round of crises, will provide enough incentives to the East Asian countries to reach agreement on institutionalizing the CMI by increasing swap amounts and the number of swaps, and creating an efficient regional surveillance mechanism.

Stage two: a common basket of currencies as a numeraire

Once the foundation for financial market stability is laid and the mechanism for policy coordination is put in place, East Asian countries will find it easier to consider introducing alternative collective exchange rate regimes, including common pegging to a currency basket and an Asian version of the European Monetary System (EMS).

The first step for stage two is to identify a managed exchange rate system that is acceptable to a large number of countries in the region. One potential candidate is a common basket peg system, with a wider band first, and then a narrow band. The currency weights can be roughly equal to trade weights. The yen can be one of the three major currencies in the basket, since it has been independently floating against the dollar and the euro.

Williamson (1999) suggested the adoption of a common basket of major currencies as a reference rate or numeraire to be used in the formulation of exchange rate policy among Asian countries (e.g., ACU). He does not necessarily advocate a hard peg to the common basket, which he considers to be as impractical as the creation of an ERM would be in Asia right now.

Before moving on to tight pegging, which is likely to require a long period of preparation and negotiation, Asian countries may first attempt to adopt a common unit of account for the conduct of exchange rate policy while maintaining a variety of exchange rate arrangements, including intermediate regimes and a currency board. Williamson (1999) argues that this alone would be a positive development for monetary integration. This is because the common unit of account may tend to create the expectation that variations in bilateral exchange rates among the dollar, yen, and euro should not affect the relative competitive positions of the countries in the region.

The most serious difficulty with managing the ACU is that, except for Malaysia, ASEAN-5 as well as Korea and Taipei,China have been floating freely, although policymakers in these countries have been intervening extensively in their foreign exchange markets. While in theory Williamson's proposal may be appealing, the ACU is not free from institutional constraints that will make it inoperable at least in the eyes of many foreign exchange market participants. Even if participating countries could agree to the ACU, a major undertaking is needed to create an enforcement mechanism that could monitor whether member countries rely on a common numeraire for their exchange rate policies. Even when member countries are bound by a multilateral agreement, in reality it would be difficult to agree on a set of criteria by which adherence to the basket as a numeraire in managing exchange rate policy could be ascertained.

Many countries, particularly small ones, may wish to stabilize their nominal as well as real effective exchange rates by loosely pegging their currencies to a basket consisting of the dollar, yen, and euro. However, the composition as well as the weights of the currencies included in the baskets would differ from country to country, given the differences in their patterns of trade. Intra-regional effective exchange rates would then remain as unstable as they are now. The countries joining in region-wide efforts to integrate financial markets may agree to switch to common basket pegging at some future date, but few countries would be inclined to adopt a common reference rate voluntarily. In particular, unless the CMI is developed into a credible regional financing mechanism, ASEAN+3 would not be easily persuaded to agree to a common reference rate. The reason is that, unless they are assured of short-term financing for balance-of-payments imbalances, they would not even partially give up their monetary independence.

Stage three: pegging to a common basket

After a period of successful experimentation with the ACU, the CMI countries could move to pegging to a common basket to stabilize intraregional effective exchange rates. Stability of the intraregional exchange rate will reduce costs related to exchange rate volatility and in so doing promote intraregional trade. Each participating country will also find it easier to stabilize its real effective exchange rate. For the region as a whole, such a system would insulate it from fluctuations in the value of the dollar against other major currencies, in particular from the impact of the variability of the dollar/yen exchange rate.

The basket pegging system for East Asia advocated by Williamson (1999) is consistent with a wide variety of exchange rate regimes with different degrees of "fixedness." It only rules out free floating. In the East Asian context, the pegging system raises two issues: whether the peg should be fixed or crawling and how wide the band of fluctuation should be. As for the first issue, the countries would be better-off if they chose a crawling band since they are likely to have to contend with the Balassa-Samuelson effect, which predicts real exchange rate appreciation for high-growth economies. A crawling peg may be more effective in achieving a desired rate of inflation, but is susceptible to speculative attacks. Therefore, the choice is between a wide band and an upward crawling peg, as argued by Wyplosz (2002).

If the countries decide to choose a band system, they would find it in their interest to adopt a relatively wide band. The 1997–1998 crisis showed that capital flows often display a boom-bust cycle and can be a source of overvaluation. A wide band would be more effective in responding to unexpected changes in capital flows. However, with a wide band, the pegging system would undermine its main objective of stabilizing effective exchange rates among regional currencies. Since one cannot determine a priori an optimal band, a better strategy would be to start with a wide band and then gradually move to a narrow one, as the market participants' confidence builds up.

However, as Wyplosz points out, this sequencing may entail a serious danger in that when they are confident, policymakers often fail to detect changes in market sentiment signaling impending danger, leaving themselves vulnerable to speculative attacks. To avoid these problems, the period of pegging with a narrow band should be relatively short, with the clear understanding that pegging is a temporary regime on the way to monetary union.

Eichengreen and Bayoumi (1999) also point out that defending a common peg would be much more difficult than introducing it. Success in defense requires an efficient institutional framework to promote (i) policy coordination among the participating member countries, (ii) a financing mechanism that will provide financial resources to the exchange rates of weak-currency members, and (iii) a surveillance mechanism that could impose policy conditionality on the countries receiving the financial support. In the absence of these institutional arrangements, a tight common peg could create an Asian version of the Snake, not the EMS.

Another critical defect of the basket system is that the three major currencies in the basket are not part of the exchange rate arrangement designed to promote financial integration. There is no—and will not be in the future—commitment to unlimited interventions from the central banks of the three currencies in the basket. In the absence of such a commitment, the basket approach with the bilateral swap arrangement (BSA) of the CMI would not be able to withstand determined speculation.

In the common pegging scheme, as with the US and EU, Japan will remain outside of the regional exchange rate arrangement; that is, the yen will continue to float against the East Asian common basket. Although Japan is expected to play a key role in the region's efforts to promote financial and monetary integration, it is not required or prepared to intervene to sustain the pegging in other Asian countries. In the absence of Japan's direct participation, the common basket pegging may delay monetary integration between Japan and the rest of the region. For these reasons, the period of hard pegging to the three-currency basket should be relatively short. It should be recognized that it is a short-term arrangement to be succeeded by the Asian Monetary System (AMS) at the next stage.

Stage four: establishing an Asian monetary system

If the ratio of intraregional trade involving Japan and the weight of the yen in the currency basket increase as expected, the correlation between the other Asian currencies and the yen will also increase. Then the economic conditions would be ripe for including the yen as an integral part of a collective exchange rate system rather than keeping it outside. This could be achieved by shifting to an ERM like that in Europe.

One might indeed argue that moving from a basket peg to an AMS that includes Japan is easier than moving from the current system of diverse exchange rate arrangements to a common pegging system. However, it is not clear whether and under what conditions Japan could fix its bilateral exchange rates against other East Asian currencies unless the yen plays the role of a dominant currency. Wyplosz (2002) points out that common basket pegging with the BSAs may perpetuate Asia's tradition of eschewing institution building. Failure to build regional collective institutions including a financing system may in the end delay building the foundation of a currency union. Even if the East Asian countries could agree to common pegging, the system would be vulnerable to speculative attacks unless it could be tied down with expectations that they would succeed in creating a CCA in the future.

A regime shift from pegging to a common basket of currencies to a system in which bilateral exchange rates among the member countries are tightly fixed as in the ERM is a decision that requires collective actions on institution building at the regional level. Operating an AMS requires creating a new monetary unit similar to the ECU whose value will be tied to a basket of specified amounts of Asian currencies. The members of the AMS will also have to establish an Asian version of the European Monetary Cooperation Fund (EMCF). The bilateral swap system under the CMI as it is structured is a far cry from the EMCF.

The Asian ERM may be impractical because the foreign exchange markets in some of the countries are not well developed, so that effective intervention to defend the cross rates in other participating countries may not be easy. Further, differences in trade patterns and the diversity of preferences with regard to exchange rate regimes and inflation rates may not allow a system as tight as the ERM.

There is also the problem of including the yen in the system. Because of the super economy status of Japan, the yen is likely to emerge as the dominant currency, as the German mark did in the EMS. The yen's dominance may induce other Asian countries to fix their currencies to it and therefore result in the creation of a de facto yen bloc in the region.

The EMS was sustainable in part because it was endowed with unlimited financial support along with capital controls in the weak-currency countries (Wyplosz 2002). In contrast, the amount of financing available through the CMI-BSA is so small that it can hardly send a clear message to the market that any speculative attempt to break off one currency from others in the region will end up in failure. This is because there is no collective commitment to provide unlimited support to fend off such speculation. The preceding discussion once again underscores the importance of enlarging and institutionalizing the CMI to promote a successful collective regional exchange rate arrangement in East Asia.

Stage five: establishing a common currency area

After successful management of an Asian version of the ERM, during which a plan for adopting a common currency is prepared, the countries of the region may emulate the European experience of monetary integration by taking steps to build requisite institutions, harmonize policies, and introduce common standards and codes.

As noted earlier, the creation of a CCA is the most critical economic and political step to take and as such requires careful preparation to mitigate the undesirable consequences of abruptly adopting a common currency. Although the European experience suggests that economic criteria for a successful CCA are not as important as they are claimed to be, the last stage of monetary integration requires a large number of agreements that will erode national sovereignty, together with the loss of independent monetary policy. The final preparations should include harmonization of standards of banking, accounting, and the financial regulatory system; the rules of seigniorage sharing; and the provision of central bank functions. As Wyplosz (2002) points out, creating a central bank is bound to raise delicate issues of delegation of authority and democratic accountability. Given the heterogeneous political systems and levels of economic development of countries in the region, these issues will be the most serious obstacles to overcome on the way to monetary integration. However, the regional cooperation and integration process has just begun, and the economic environment is changing fast. Convergence in economic development is taking place quickly and the political will for cooperation is increasing. We are hopeful that East Asia is now at the starting point in a long process of regional economic and financial integration, just as Europe was several decades ago.

References

Alesina, A., and R. J. Barro. 2002. Currency Unions, *Quarterly Journal of Economics* 117 (2): 409–436.

Alesina, A., R. J. Barro, and S. Tenreyro. 2002. Optimal Currency Areas. NBER Macroeconomics Annual.

Bayoumi, T., and B. Eichengreen. 1993. Shocking Aspects of European Monetary Integration. In *Adjustment and Growth in the European Monetary Union,* edited by Francisco Torres and Francesco Givavazzi, 193–229. Cambridge University Press.

———. 1994. One Money or Many? Analyzing the Prospects for Monetary Unification in Various Parts of the World. *Studies in International Finance* no. 76. Princeton University Press.

———. 1999. Is Asia an Optimum Currency Area? Can it Become One? Regional, Global and Historical Perspectives on Asian Monetary Relations. In *Exchange Rate Policies in Emerging Asian Countries,* edited by Stefan Collignon, Jean Pisani-Ferry, and Yung Chul Park, 347–366. London: Routledge.

Blanchard, Olivier J., and D. Quah. 1989. The Dynamic Effects of Aggregate Demand and Supply Disturbances. *American Economic Review* (September): 655–673.

Broda, C. 2001. Coping with Terms of Trade Shocks: Pegs and Float. *American Economic Review* 91 (2): 376–380.

Calvo, Guillermo A., and Carmen M. Reinhart. 2002. Fear of Floating, *Quarterly Journal of Economics* 117 (2): 379–408.

Crockett, Andrew. 1994. Monetary Policy Implications of Increased Capital Flows, Changing Capital Markets: Implications for Monetary Policy. Symposium sponsored by Federal Reserve Bank of Kansas City, Jackson Hole, August 1993.

Eichengreen, B. 1994. *International Monetary Arrangements for the 21st Century*. Washington, DC: Brookings Institution.

———. 1999. *Toward a New Financial Architecture: A Practical Post-Asia Agenda*. Washington, DC: Institute for International Economics.

Fischer, S. 2001. Exchange Rate Regimes: Is the Bipolar View Correct? *Journal of Economic Perspectives* 15 (2): 3–24.

Frankel, J. 1999. No Single Exchange Rate Regime is Right for All Countries or at All Times. Graham Lecture, Essays in International Finance no. 215. Princeton: Princeton University Press.

Frankel, J., and A. Rose. 1998. The Endogeneity of the Optimum Currency Area Criteria. *Economic Journal* 108: 1009–1025.

———. 2002. An Estimate of the Effect of Common Currencies on Trade and Income. *Quarterly Journal of Economics* 117 (2): 437–466.

Frankel, J., S. Schmukler, and L. Servén. 2000. Verifiability and the Vanishing Intermediate Exchange Rate Regime. In *Brookings Trade Forum 2000*, edited by S. Collins and D. Rodrik. Washington, DC: Brookings Institution.

Frankel, J., and Shang-Jin Wei. 1994. Yen Bloc or Dollar Bloc? Exchange Rate Policies of the East Asian Economies. In *Macroeconomic Linkages: Savings, Exchange Rates, and Capital Flows*, edited by Takatoshi Ito and Anne Krueger. NBER-East Asia Seminar on Economics, Vol. 3. University of Chicago Press.

Hausmann, R., U. Panizza, and E. Stein. 2000. Why Do Countries Float the Way They Float? Washington, DC: Inter-American Development Bank. (mimeo.)

Helliwell, J. 1998. *How Much Do National Borders Matter?* Brookings Institution.

Ito, T. 2000. Principal Causes of Asian Export Deceleration. In *Asian Exports*, edited by Dilip Das, 75–114. ADB-Oxford University Press.

Ito, T., E. Ogawa, and Y. Sasaki. 1998. How Did the Dollar Peg Fail in Asia? *Journal of the Japanese and International Economies* 12: 256–304.

Kaminsky, G. L., and C. M. Reinhart. 1999. The Twin Crises: The Causes of Banking and Balance of Payments Problems. *American Economic Review* 89 (3): 473–500.

Krugman, P. 1989. *Exchange-Rate Instability*. Cambridge, MA: MIT Press.

Kydland, F., and E. Prescott. 1977. Rules Rather than Discretion: The Inconsistency of Optimal Plans. *Journal of Political Economy* 85: 473–491.

McKinnon, R. 1963. Optimum Currency Areas. *American Economic Review* 53 (September): 717–724.

Mundell, R. 1961. A Theory of Optimum Currency Areas. *American Economic Review* 51 (November): 509–517.

Mussa, M., P. Masson, A. Swoboda, E. Jadresic, P. Mauro, and A. Berg. 2000. *Exchange Rate Regimes in an Increasingly Integrated World Economy*. Washington, DC: International Monetary Fund.

Obstfeld, M., and K. Rogoff. 1995. The Mirage of Fixed Exchange Rate. NBER Working Paper no. 5191.

Ogawa, E., and T. Ito. 2002. On the Desirability of a Regional Basket Currency Arrangement. *Journal of the Japanese and International Economies* 16 (September): 317–334.

Ogawa, E., and L. Sun. 2001. How Were Capital Inflows Stimulated under the Dollar Peg System? In *Regional and Global Capital Flows: Macroeconomic Causes and Consequences*, edited by T. Ito and A. O. Krueger. Chicago: University of Chicago Press.

Pozo, S. 1992. Conditional Exchange-Rate Volatility and the Volume of International Trade: Evidence from the Early 1990s. *The Review of Economics and Statistics* 74 (2): 325–329.

Rose, A. 2000. One Money, One Market: Estimating the Effect of Common Currencies on Trade. *Economic Policy* 30: 7–46.

Rose, A., and C. Engel. 2001. Currency Unions and International Integration. NBER Working Paper no. 7872, September.

Rose, A., and E. van Wincoop. 2001. National Money as a Barrier to International Trade: The Real Case for Currency Union. *American Economic Review* 91 (2): 386–390.

Sasaki, Y. N. 2002. Doru Peggu tai Basuketto Peggu [Dollar Peg versus Basket Peg]. In Kinyu no Atarashii Nagare, edited by Katsumi Matsuura and Yasuhiro Yonezawa. Tokyo: Nihon Hyoron Sha.

Sato, K., Z. Zhang, and M. McAleer. 2001. Is East Asia an Optimum Currency Area? Paper Prepared for the 2001 Far Eastern Meeting of the Econometric Society, Kobe.

Stock, J. H., and N. W. Watson. 1991. A Probability Model of Coincident Economic Indicators. In *Leading Economic Indicators: New Approaches and Forecasting Records,* edited by K. Lahiri and G. H. Moore, 63–89. UK: Cambridge University Press.

Summers, L. 1999. Testimony before the Senate Foreign Relations Subcommittee on International Economic Policy and Export/Trade Promotion, 27 January.

Tenreyro, S. 2002. Economic Effects of Currency Unions. Harvard University, March. (unpublished)

Williamson, J. 1999. The Case for a Common Basket Peg for East Asian Countries. In *Exchange Rate Policies in Emerging Asian Countries,* edited by Stefan Collignon, Jean Pisani-Ferry, and Yung Chul Park, 327–343. London: Routledge.

———. 2000a. *Exchange Rate Regimes of Emerging Markets: Reviving the Intermediate Option*. Washington, DC: Institute for International Economics.

———. 2000b. Designing a Middle Way Between Fixed and Flexible Exchange Rates. Paper Presented at a Conference on Monetary and Exchange Rate Policies: Options for Egypt, Organized by the Egyptian Center for Economic Studies in Cairo, Institute for International Economics.

Wyplosz, C. 1997. EMU: Why and How It Might Happen. *Journal of Economic Perspectives* 11(4): 3–22.

———. 2000. *Exchange Rate Regimes: Some Lessons from Postwar Europe*. Washington, DC: Group of Thirty.

———. 2002. Fiscal Policy: Institutions vs. Rules. CEPR Discussion Paper no. 3238. http://www.cepr.org/pubs/dps/DP3238.asp.

Yoshino, N., S. Kaji, and A. Suzuki. 2001. The Basket-Peg, Dollar-Peg and Floating: A Comparative Analysis of Exchange Rate Regimes. (mimeo.)